Delaine's copy

A Child's Garden of Standards

Linking School Gardens to California Education Standards • Grades Two Through Six

Publishing Information

A Child's Garden of Standards: Linking School Gardens to California Education Standards was supported by the Nutrition Services Division, California Department of Education. It was edited by Janice Lowen Agee, Office of the State Superintendent of Public Instruction, and Sheila Bruton, CDE Press, working in cooperation with Phoebe Tanner, Visiting Educator, Nutrition Services Division. It was prepared for printing by the staff of CDE Press: it was designed by Cheryl McDonald and was typeset by Carey Johnson. It was published by the Department, 1430 N Street, Sacramento, California (mailing address: P.O. Box 944272, Sacramento, CA 94244-2720). It was distributed under the provisions of the Library Distribution Act and *Government Code* Section 11096.

ISBN 0-8011-1579-5

Ordering Information

Copies of this publication are available for $17.50 each, plus shipping and handling charges. California residents are charged sales tax. Orders may be sent to the California Department of Education, CDE Press, Sales Office, P.O. Box 271, Sacramento, CA 95812-0271; FAX (916) 323-0823. Prices on all publications are subject to change.

In addition, an illustrated *Educational Resources Catalog* describing publications, videos, and other instructional media available from the Department can be obtained without charge by writing to the address given above or by calling the Sales Office at (916) 445-1260 or (800) 995-4099.

Photo Credits

The California Department of Education gratefully acknowledges the following persons and organizations for the use of the photographs that appear in this publication: Kelsey Siegel, cover (top left), xviii; Joann Osburn, cover (top right); Teri Hawkins, cover (bottom), 15; Elizabeth C. Price, vii, ix; Stephanie Rausser, viii; Phoebe Tanner, x, xxiii, 69; Ann M. Evans, xii, 31; Kay O'Neill, xiii; Theresa Tower, xiv; Cassie Scott, xvii; K. C. Deichler, xx; Wendy McPhetridge, xxii; Tyler/Center for Ecoliteracy, xxiv, 50; Clemmie J. Watson, 1; Diane Swanson, 14, 32; *Sacramento Bee*/ Lezlie Sterling, 68. All photographs used by permission.

Prepared for publication
by CSEA members.

CONTENTS

MESSAGE FROM THE STATE SUPERINTENDENT OF PUBLIC INSTRUCTION

When I first called for a garden in every California school in 1995, I knew educators would respond because I had witnessed the transformation that occurs with students and teachers in their school gardens. I had seen these individuals' curiosity, imagination, and thirst for learning magnified as they nurtured life from seed to table. What I did not know was how relevant gardens would become to the educational challenges that have emerged since then.

Garden-based education is well grounded in the writings of educators, such as Rousseau, Thomas Jefferson, John Dewey, and Howard Gardner. As restauranteur Alice Waters, a former Montessori schoolteacher, has also so aptly observed, "From the garden, and the kitchen, and the table, you learn empathy—from each other and for all creation; and you learn patience and self-discipline. A curriculum that teaches these lessons gives children an orientation to the future—it can give them hope."

After standards in the core academic subjects were adopted in 1997 and 1998, some people became concerned that time in the garden would not be valued because classroom time was at a premium. Although I was a leading advocate of standards in order to ensure a higher quality education for all our children and to keep California's economy competitive, I increasingly recognize there is a danger that the standards will become a series of rote lessons. A garden in every school is even more essential to make our standards come alive. We must not lose the creativity, problem solving, and sheer love of learning that comes from hands-on, experiential learning.

Gardens should not compete with our standards; gardens should be an avenue to high standards. Together with community members and support from the agricultural community, educators are overcoming many of the physical and logistical barriers to establishing gardens. However, California teachers and administrators still need our support in ensuring that they are able to link the school garden to the standards. Thus the idea for this document, *A Child's Garden of Standards,* was born.

Since 1995 my vision for a garden in every school has expanded to include providing garden-fresh fruit and vegetables and nutritious meals in the cafeteria, recycling lunch waste, cooking in the classroom, and visiting local farms. Widening the circle of learning from the school garden to local farms provides a context for students to understand California family farming and agriculture as well as the environment they will inherit.

Gardens also offer families a way to participate in school life. Some families, particularly those from other countries, may feel uncomfortable when asked to help out at school because their English skills or educational background do not give them a solid classroom footing. For these families the living classroom of a garden can be a much more inviting environment in which to engage in their children's education.

The recent epidemic of obesity and related diseases in school-age children also reinforces the need to make a garden in every school an essential part of the learning environment. School gardens play a role in reversing this trend toward obesity when linked with fresh vegetables and fruit served in the cafeteria and nutrition education provided in the classroom.

Therefore, the California Department of Education published *Nutrition to Grow On*, an activity guide that links nutrition education to garden-based education, and *Kids Cook Farm-Fresh Food,* which features profiles of California family farmers and recipes suitable for the classroom. *A Child's Garden of Standards* looks at these two earlier documents, along with nine other instructional materials, and links specific activities to standards in science, history–social science, mathematics, and English–language arts.

Several tasks are still undone with respect to garden-based education. I join educators, agriculturalists, environmentalists, and others in calling for more research from our schools of education to help us quantify the results of garden-based education. I also join them in calling for more curricula to be developed that fully integrate garden-based education into the core academic subjects and resources.

I am a devoted gardener, home cook, and recycler. I hope teachers throughout California will find this publication a useful guide for linking the garden to a cohesive educational program. This document, coupled with common sense when one sees first-hand in the garden the wonder on a student's face, will surely make garden-based education a solid partner in our educational enterprise in the decades to come.

Delaine Eastin

DELAINE EASTIN
State Superintendent of Public Instruction

ACKNOWLEDGMENTS

The California Department of Education (CDE) collaborated with staff of the University of California at Davis Children's Garden Program and the Occidental Arts and Ecology Center to make this guide a reality. The University of California Division of Agriculture and Natural Resources provided additional financial support and feedback throughout the process.

The Department gratefully acknowledges the extensive efforts of Cynthia Havstad and Carol Hillhouse of the University of California at Davis Children's Garden Program, School Gardens Project. Along with Phoebe Tanner, CDE Visiting Educator and teacher at Martin Luther King Middle School and the Edible Schoolyard in Berkeley, they developed and clarified the concepts and methods that are presented in the guide for using existing garden-based education instructional materials to teach California's academic content standards.

The following educators with extensive experience in school gardens reviewed the instructional materials and lessons that support the content standards: Cherie Barnecut, Rick Blacker, Jamie Buffington, Marika Bergsund, Kitty Connelly, Sheri Klittich, Erika Perloff, Ashley Nelson, Yvonne Savio, Beth Sonnenberg, Deanna Stratton, Linda Whent, and Marge Wright. In addition, Tina Poles from the Occidental Arts and Ecology Center made significant contributions of time, creativity, and leadership.

Students need to be aware of the world around them, aware of the consequences of what they eat, aware of our precious natural resources. The school garden can communicate these important lessons.

Alice Waters
Chez Panisse, Owner
Edible Schoolyard, Founder
M. L. King Middle School
Berkeley Unified School District

The following people devoted time to reviewing drafts of the guide: Ronda Adams, Cherie Barnecut, Rick Blacker, Dan Desmond, Dee Desmond, Pam Emery, Rich Engel, Kelly Goughner, Phil Lafontaine, Jean Landeen, Ralphene Lee, Holiday Matchett, Erika Perloff, Beth Sonnenberg, Deanna Stratton, Deborah Tucker, and Marge Wright. Their suggestions, large and small, were very much appreciated and have improved the final product immeasurably.

The guide would not have been possible without the vision and backing of Marilyn Briggs, Director of the Nutrition Services Division at CDE. Several CDE Garden Team members played significant roles: Deborah Tamannaie shepherded the project in its early stages; Ann M. Evans assisted in moving the document from an idea to its publication; and Margaret Aumann, Deborah Beall, and Mary Lussier provided additional assistance. Janice DeBenedetti, Manager of the Home Economics Careers and Technology Unit, also offered support.

Mark Van Horn, James Steichel, Raoul Adamchak, and Tree Kilpatrick at the University of California at Davis Plant Science Teaching Center and Student Farm provided inspiration that has been essential to the completion of this project.

Finally, the publication of this document would have not been possible without the guidance and editing expertise of Janice Lowen Agee, Executive Editor in the Office of the State Superintendent of Public Instruction.

This guide, *A Child's Garden of Standards: Linking School Gardens to California Education Standards,* is designed to show how garden-based education (GBE) strongly supports the state's academic content standards. Although it is not a curriculum, the guide bridges the distance between the garden experience and the standards by linking specific lessons to specific standards for grades two through six.

The Success of School Gardens

School gardens are flourishing across California. In a survey conducted in 2002, about 2,400 schools reported having gardens. Each garden is unique, its character shaped by the place and the people who garden there.

At Grant Elementary School in Santa Monica, first- and second-grade students eat artichokes, broccoli, carrots, chard, beets, and peas they have grown in planter boxes outside the classroom door. In a one-acre garden at Pixley Union School in the Central Valley, students, teachers, and food service staff grow watermelons, corn, tomatoes, onions, cucumbers, and strawberries for the school salad bar. And at the Second Street Elementary School garden, wedged among three Los Angeles freeways, students keep records of the numerous species of butterflies that visit. Different as they are from

one another, school gardens are all places where learning converges with beauty, fun, work, and discovery.

There are as many good reasons for the popularity of school gardens as there are gardens themselves. Although relatively few evaluations of school garden programs have been conducted, educators suggest and research indicates the following findings as among the most compelling results of garden-based education:

- Gardens integrate various disciplines and bring meaning to the standards for science, history–social science, mathematics, and English–language arts.
- Children who grow vegetables in school gardens are more willing to taste and eat vegetables than children who do not have access to school gardens. The willingness to eat vegetables is a critical step in developing healthy eating patterns and is especially important today in light of the current epidemic of childhood obesity.
- Students with all levels of skills, varied learning styles, and diverse backgrounds can find a common interest in a school

---

Freeway sounds fade into the distance, the sun is brilliant, the soil is moist, plants whisper secrets of the centuries until suddenly a shout interrupts the silence, "I found one!" A young scientist collects the butterfly egg on its host plant and carefully places the plant in a jar of water and then into a rearing cage.

Our school is a quarter of a mile from downtown Los Angeles and is bordered on three sides by freeways. Our garden provides a home for 16 species of butterflies and more than 18 species of birds and is now registered as a National Wildlife Federation "school habitat."

The California standards declare that students in first through third grades should learn how to use simple tools to measure weather conditions and record daily and seasonal changes. Students should know that plants and animals have predictable life cycles, that their adaptations and behaviors enhance survival, and that organisms depend on one another and the environment for survival. A garden is an ideal place to teach these concepts. Through garden education we can reconnect ourselves to the past, look forward to a lush, ripe future, and fully experience the state standards and science concepts. Garden language is universal.

Brandyn Scully, Teacher
Second Street Elementary School
Los Angeles Unified School District
Los Angeles

garden. Students who struggle in the classroom frequently find success in the school garden experience. Often the number of classroom discipline problems is reduced.

- Students learn responsibility and develop life skills through their work in gardens. They cooperate to finish a job and learn to respect the contributions of others. They have the opportunity to take pleasure in physical work.
- Gardens educate students to use their senses. They give children the opportunity to experience the natural world through sight, sound, smell, touch, and taste.
- Gardens connect students to the earth and ecological processes and provide them with empowering experiences as they explore environmental questions.
- Gardening provides an avenue for the community to contribute to education. For example, immigrant parents or senior citizens, who may otherwise feel uncomfortable at schools, draw on agrarian or home gardening experience to participate in garden programs. Local businesses or organizations have a vital and visible recipient for their contributions.
- Successful gardens strengthen school pride and identity. Older children can instruct younger children and interact in a way that is constructive to both.

School Gardens and the Academic Content Standards

With the state's adoption of academic content standards in science, history–social science, mathematics, and English–language arts in 1997 and 1998, California joined a nationwide movement toward standards-based education. Currently, 49 states have academic standards in place. The California content standards define what students need to learn at each grade level from kindergarten through grade twelve. Standards are intended to ensure that a particular level of rigor is maintained and that the same concepts are being taught in all classrooms at each grade level, whether the classes are across the hall from each other or at opposite ends of the state.

Standards determine *what* and *when* concepts are to be taught; they do not dictate *how* they will be taught. The *how* is left to teachers, schools, and school districts. The opportunity to select instructional materials and determine instructional strategies opens the door to the use of school gardens.

In addition to demonstrating academic concepts, the garden is a wonderful investment in building social capital among students. Through planting, caring for, and harvesting the various items and finally sitting down to share a meal, students build and strengthen relationships. The garden is a shared effort that yields not only nutrition for the physical body but also nourishment for the soul. We do learn it when we live it . . . and students without question do too!

Judy Moon, Home Economics Careers and Technology Teacher
Mt. Diablo High School
Mt. Diablo Unified School District
Concord

For one final moment in our evolution as a nation, we still have a community memory of the family farm. My hope is that educators working with children in school gardens understand that they are giving memories to the children. They are giving them a touchstone to the past.

David Mas Masumoto,
Author and Farmer
Del Rey

Although some people fear that standards-based education creates a barrier to teaching in school gardens, the garden experience can be a vital partner with the standards. On the one hand gardening brings life to the standards. The garden provides a full context in which to explore, connect, and expand concepts in the standards. On the other hand the potential for learning through the garden, rich as it is, cannot be realized for many students unless coupled with the explicit instruction and clear connections that the standards can provide.

In addition, GBE naturally crosses subject areas, providing an integrated learning experience that is analogous to real-world experiences. Teachers can connect the act of growing food to multiple standards; this integration captivates the mind and encourages the development of lifelong learners.

The Seed-to-Table Concept

Many educators are building successful garden programs around an integrated perspective that is becoming known as "seed-to-table." This concept includes the experience and understanding involved in the acts of planting, harvesting, preparing, and eating food and in recycling food waste. The seed-to-table process for school garden programs can be divided into five general content areas: *gardening, nutrition, cooking, waste management,* and *agricultural systems. Agricultural systems* involves the study of agriculture and of the resources required for crop production. This topic is distinct from *gardening* in that it deals with large-scale production and distribution of crops.

An example of the seed-to-table concept in action is a school garden program in which students grow vegetables and then harvest, prepare, and eat the vegetables. Students also sort their lunchtime waste, compost it appropriately, and use the finished compost to feed the soil in the garden. In addition, they might learn how a local farmer would grow the same vegetables. The seed-to-table concept is powerful because children and adults experience the nurturing aspects of gardening and eating together and, in doing so, begin to understand better the complexities of food production.

School garden programs often also involve nonfood plants. Gardens may contain plants that provide habitat for insects or birds; inedible native plants; or plants used for making clothing, dyes, or rope. These nonfood plants broaden students' opportunities to learn from their garden experience.

The main purpose of *A Child's Garden of Standards* is to demonstrate that garden-based education (GBE) strongly supports and enhances California's academic content standards. Most of the suggested activities in this guide come from 11 GBE instructional materials. The tables for grades two through six are the heart of the document. They provide an easy way for educators to identify grade-appropriate, garden-based activities in each core subject area and help educators focus their programs on one or more of the seed-to-table content areas: gardening, nutrition, cooking, waste management, and agricultural systems.

Intended Audience

The guide was written with several audiences in mind. First, it is for teachers with interest and enthusiasm but little or no experience in garden-based activities. Second, it is for teachers who currently use gardens and are looking for new ideas and resources. Third, it is for school administrators, such as superintendents, principals, and school board members, who want to gain a general understanding of how a school garden fits into their educational goals. And finally, it is for the countless volunteers and nonteacher professionals, such as families,

Awareness is the first word that enters my mind when I reflect on the impact of our school garden on the children. Now they take time out to eat, they celebrate food with a harvest of the garden, they understand and feel the benefits of eating vegetables. The most memorable quote was made by one of my first graders after visiting the garden for the first time when we talked about how things grow in the garden, "Ms. Tower, can we visit the garden again so we can grow?"

Theresa Tower, Teacher
Pennekamp Elementary School
Manhattan Beach Unified School District
Manhattan Beach

Master Gardeners, and nutritionists, who play a crucial role in making school garden programs thrive in California.

Instructional Materials Used in the Guide

Most GBE materials span the levels kindergarten through grade six. Some materials have been aligned to the California standards in the four core academic subject areas, and the number of such materials is growing as authors and publishers realize the importance of the standards. However, many materials were written before the standards were completed. Some may cover a topic that is addressed by a standard at a particular grade level, but they are written with a complexity or terminology appropriate for another grade level. For this reason a variety of different but complementary materials were selected for use in this guide (see Table 1). If the standards can be supported by GBE but the materials have no such activities, the tables provide suggestions for general activities.

The following questions guided the selection of the instructional materials used in the guide:

- Which academic subject areas do the instructional material's activities address? Does this teaching material, taken with others, help cover all four core academic subject areas?
- Which seed-to-table content area does the instructional material address? Does the material, taken with others, help to cover all the content areas?
- Which grade level does the material teach? Does it, taken with others, help to cover grades two through six?
- How widely used is the instructional material? Is it readily available and affordable?
- Is the instructional material aligned by the author or publisher to the California standards in the core academic subject areas?
- Is the material current?

Although this guide covers GBE activities only for grades two through six, that does not mean that GBE is inappropriate for kindergarten and first-grade students or that middle and high school students are too old for gardens. The focus here is on grades two through six because in kindergarten through the first grade the lack of clearly stated connections to the standards does not deter teachers from GBE as may often happen at the later elementary grade levels. Fewer

Table 1 The Instructional Materials Used in the Guide

Instructional Material	Publisher	Suggested Grade Levels	Seed-to-table Content Area	Brief Description
Simple and Complex Machines Used in Agriculture *Fruits and Vegetables for Health* *What's Bugging You?*	California Foundation for Agriculture in the Classroom (CFAITC) 2300 River Plaza Dr. Sacramento, CA 95833 800-700-2482 *www.cfaitc.org*	2–5 4–6 4–6	Agricultural systems Nutrition Agricultural systems Gardening Agricultural systems	These lessons are three of the many lessons available from CFAITC. All lessons are available on its Web site and can be downloaded individually. Lessons cover a broad range of agricultural topics, including insects, genetics, farm machinery, and edible plant parts. CFAITC provides teacher training, crop information sheets, a newsletter, and a teacher resource guide.
Closing the Loop (2000)	California Integrated Waste Management (CIWMB) Accounting Unit P.O. Box 4025 Sacramento, CA 95812 916-341-6769 *www.ciwmb.ca.gov*	K–6	Waste management	Fifty lessons are organized into two modules: K–3 and 4–6. The activities introduce students to integrated waste management. Units cover nutrient cycles, resource conservation, and waste reduction, including composting and vermicomposting. CIWMB provides teacher training.
The Growing Classroom (1990)	Life Lab 1156 High Street Santa Cruz, CA 95064 831-459-2001 *www.lifelab.org*	2–6	Gardening Waste management Agricultural systems	The guide includes over 70 hands-on garden activities. However, the nutrition lessons and case studies are out of date. Life Lab provides teacher training.
Junior Master Gardener, Level One, Teacher /Leader Guide (1999)	Junior Master Gardener (JMG) Program JMG Kids 4066 State Highway 6 South College Station, TX 77845 888-564-5437 *www.jmgkids.com*	3–5	Gardening Nutrition Cooking Waste management Agricultural systems	These 4-H youth gardening materials are designed for the regular classroom or after-school programs. Topics include soil and water, ecology/environment, horticulture, insects and diseases, landscape design, fruits, nuts, vegetables and herbs, life skills, and career explorations. Lessons are designed to support Texas Essential Knowledge and Skills. JMG provides teacher training in California with a focus on the California academic content standards.
Kids Cook Farm-Fresh Food (2002)	California Department of Education CDE Press P.O. Box 271 Sacramento, CA 95812 800-995-4099 *www.cde.ca.gov/cdepress*	2–6	Gardening Cooking Agricultural systems	Organized by season, the publication has 18 chapters. Each chapter focuses on one crop and provides a crop description, a profile of a farmer, an activity, and recipes. The emphasis is on small California farms and sustainable agriculture. Recipes are designed around seasonal, fresh foods.
Nutrition to Grow On (2001)	California Department of Education CDE Press P.O. Box 271 Sacramento, CA 95812 800-995-4099 *www.cde.ca.gov/cdepress*	4–6	Gardening Nutrition Cooking Waste management	Nine nutrition lessons are each integrated with a corresponding garden activity. Lessons focus on the Food Guide Pyramid, nutrients needed for life, portion size, exercise, personal goal settings, and advertising.

Continued on next page

Table 1 (Continued)

Instructional Material	Publisher	Suggested Grade Levels	Seed-to-table Content Area	Brief Description
Project Food, Land & People: Resources for Learning (2000)	Project Food, Land & People Presidio of San Francisco P.O. Box 29474 San Francisco, CA 94129 *www.foodlandpeople.org*	K–12	Gardening Nutrition Cooking Waste management Agricultural systems	These 55 lessons are designed to show the interdependence of agriculture, the environment, and human needs. Topics include growing seedlings, nutrition, health, seasonal celebrations, land use, and population growth. Twenty lessons are available in Spanish. The project provides training.
TWIGS Youth Development Program (1997)	University of California Cooperative Extension San Mateo and San Francisco 625 Miramontes St., Suite 200 Half Moon Bay, CA 94019 650-726-9059	K–6	Gardening Nutrition Cooking Waste management	Fifteen basic gardening lessons and 15 cooking/nutrition lessons are designed for use in classroom or after-school programs. The program connects gardening and nutrition to influence children's attitudes and food choices.
Worms Eat Our Garbage: Classroom Activities for a Better Environment (1993)	Flower Press 10332 Shaver Road Kalamazoo, MI 49024 269-327-0108 *www.wormwoman.com*	4–8	Gardening Waste management	More than 100 lessons focus on the world of worms, vermicomposting, and beyond the worm bin. Activities address a broad range of math and English-language arts standards.

teaching materials are available for grades seven through twelve, so additional instructional materials need to be developed.

Other excellent instructional materials are available to support GBE but are not included in the grade-level tables. Some go beyond the scope of this document, and others overlap significantly in content with materials that ultimately were included. For instance, there is a large body of environmental education materials, many of which overlap in content with garden-based materials, that are not a part of this guide. (For more information on these materials, visit the Web site <*www.creec.org*>.)

Grade-Level Tables

This guide is designed to provide the teacher with good, easy-to-implement activities that *strongly* support one or more of the content standards. The intent of the guide is not to use every activity in each material or to find an activity for every standard. For a number of standards, more than one activity is listed when the activities are complementary or offer good choices for the teacher.

Some activities listed in the guide do a good job of *applying* a standard but do not completely *teach* the content of the standard. For example, students working with recipes in *Kids Cook Farm-Fresh Food* use fractions to measure ingredients; however, the lessons do not contain instruction on the concept of fractions. Other activities cover a standard in part. Each teacher must judge the gaps and fill them appropriately.

The tables are easy to use. The title of each table indicates the grade level and subject area. The columns contain the content standards, the seed-to-table content areas addressed in the described activity, the instructional materials referenced, the suggested activities, and links to other standards. This last feature indicates whether an activity supports more than one standard. When an activity strongly supports another standard, it is also listed with the corresponding standard.

In science and history–social science, certain standards can clearly be taught more effectively than others through GBE. For those two subjects, all the GBE-related standards are listed in the tables. When no activities are indicated from the instructional materials, another

Gardening is the ultimate interdisciplinary catalyst. From science and math to history and literature, all are manifested in the art of gardening. From the sowing of the seed to the harvesting of the seed, the lessons are abundant. Whether analyzing nitrogen, phosphorous, and potassium, or synthesizing respect, responsibility, and delayed gratification, the learning happens in the head and in the hands. Doing is understanding.

Stewardship of nature, given the complex relationships in ecosystems, makes for many valuable learning opportunities. It is especially true when something goes wrong, and something invariably does. Insects, fungi, weeds, broken irrigation systems, bureaucratic roadblocks, school budgets, all present dilemmas which in turn present yet more learning opportunities.

Of course, some of my students have problems far worse than our difficulties in the garden, and I find that they sometimes turn to the patience and beauty of nature for solace.

Randy Vail, Teacher/Coordinator
The Naturalist Academy, North Hollywood High School
Los Angeles Unified School District
North Hollywood

activity is suggested to meet the standards. For example, the history–social science standards make numerous connections to agriculture, but the instructional materials make few links; therefore, general activities are suggested. Almost all standards in mathematics and English–language arts can *potentially* be supported through garden activities, but the guide lists only the standards with published activities in the instructional materials.

A limitation of these tables is that their use might result in educators gathering parts of instructional materials and delivering fragmented lessons of larger concepts. Because the tables do not include all activities from a single curriculum, there is the risk that the guide gives users many pieces of a puzzle that do not necessarily fit together to create a whole. To avoid this problem, teachers should review the entire instructional material they intend to use to understand the document's larger themes.

I believe the Edible Schoolyard has transformed King Middle School as a whole. It enriches the school in a way that nothing else does, and it does so in many ways. The impact on the curriculum is obvious. For example, students truly understand the science concepts in the seed-to-table experience through their work in the garden and in the kitchen, and they "get" the concepts in a way that a textbook cannot convey.

The Edible Schoolyard has an even greater effect on students. Working in the garden and kitchen is a bonding experience common to all students at the school, deepening their sense of community. The garden and kitchen are places where the academic hierarchy of the classroom does not apply and where every student has the opportunity to contribute meaningfully. In these places students see the results of their work, and the results are beautiful and delicious. Students experience great satisfaction and joy from their work and from a job well done, and they develop a genuine appreciation of the earth and the environment that urban kids do not get in any other way.

Neil Smith, Former Principal, M. L. King Middle School
and Current Director of Curriculum, Instruction, and Staff Development
Berkeley Unified School District
Berkeley

Academic Subjects and Garden-Based Education

This section covers general points about teaching each core academic subject through GBE.

Science

In general, the current GBE materials are strongest in science. As a means of teaching science and addressing the standards, teachers can use gardens as an outdoor laboratory in which to observe the structure and function of plants and animals, explore relationships within and between ecosystems, and witness the cycles of natural systems. Gardening is a continual exercise in investigation and experimentation, whether in formal experiments or in the informal practice of gardening in which gardeners test ideas and make adjustments. Gardens can also be used in the study of renewable and nonrenewable resources in food production. Resources and their conservation is a recurring strand that runs through both science and history–social science standards, thus integrating the two subject areas. Most important, the garden experience transforms students from observers to participants in one of life's important cycles as they plant, harvest, prepare, cook, eat, and compost food.

History–Social Science

The study of food, agriculture, and the cultures that developed alongside food production is included in the history–social science standards at all grade levels. Through gardening, students explore connections to the past and the differences between the past and the present. In California this is especially true because agriculture is a significant part of the history, the economy, and the landscape. Students bring their gardening experience to the study of current farming practices and the development of agriculture in different parts of the world. In addition, by growing food and sampling recipes from other places and different times in history, students add another dimension to the study of history–social science. Food remains one of the easiest and most pleasurable ways to experience unfamiliar ways of life and to understand the commonalities of people.

Despite the clear potential connections to history–social science standards, most garden-based instructional materials do not address the subject. For this reason the tables in this guide include suggestions for lessons that educators may develop to support history–social

I was very eager to start a garden with my students and was glad to find out that there had been one at the school at one time. When I went to see the garden, I was crushed. I saw weeds in old tires, a cement box, and lots of rocks and goatheads. I didn't know they were goatheads then, but after getting the thorns stuck in my socks along with star thistle, I definitely knew those two species.

With my class we cleaned out the cement box and found another cement box inside that one which turned out to be a perfect garden within a garden. The tires were holding a native plants garden that came alive in spring. So much for first impressions! We had a math lesson on graphing and plotting coordinates in the form of laying out our garden, so the kids didn't even know they were doing math. With the younger grades (K–3) we laid our bamboo stakes and string. Then we planted our seeds, watered them, and waited for them to germinate.

Laura Dunaj, Teacher
French Gulch-Whiskeytown Elementary School
French Gulch-Whiskeytown Union Elementary School District
French Gulch

science standards. History textbooks and instructional materials can be used to provide background information for many of the lessons.

Mathematics

Mathematics has many practical applications in a school garden. Designing, building, and measuring garden infrastructure, such as garden beds, fences, or toolsheds, are activities that can meet measurement and geometry standards. Standards on measurement, fractions, percentages, and proportions come alive through cooking. Many statistics, data analysis, and probability standards can be reinforced through manipulation of data collected from garden experiments or surveys on food preferences. Investigating mathematical relationships, such as those between various environmental

As a garden teacher I used to take each class out to the garden for weekly lessons in everything from photosynthesis to composting to nutrition. In my second-grade class there was a little boy, YJ, who had arrived from Korea two months before and had not yet spoken a word of English. He had a pal, however, who went everywhere with him. The pal, Jose, spoke for YJ. Everyone was wondering if YJ would ever say anything.

One day we were studying decomposers and discussing the beneficial insects that we find in the garden. In our efforts to find some insects, we turned over a large bale of straw, and there on the cool, damp ground were literally hundreds of squirmy and shiny "roly-polies." The students burst into squeals of excitement.

Suddenly Jose ran up to me and yelled excitedly, "Mrs. Deichler, YJ just said his first word of English!" The whole class turned and looked at us in disbelief. I said, "Well, what did he say?"

Jose explained, "Mrs. Deichler, when you turned over that bale of straw and YJ saw all those decomposers, he said, "WOW!"

This marked the beginning of YJ's speaking English. The language was there; it just took a powerful garden experience to get it moving.

Martha Deichler, Principal and Former Teacher
Vista Square Elementary School
Chula Vista Elementary School District
Chula Vista

factors and plant growth, provides teachers a means of addressing some of the algebra and function standards. Garden-based problems in statistics, measurement and geometry, and algebra and functions also offer opportunities for teachers to teach and students to apply mathematical reasoning. In general, however, garden-based materials do not emphasize mathematics, and this problem is reflected in the limited number of activities shown in the grade-level tables.

English–Language Arts

When teachers integrate English–language arts instruction into agricultural history, science, or even mathematics in the garden, students have the opportunity to apply English–language arts concepts and skills. By reading garden-related literature or conducting research in science and history, students improve their reading skills. Writing research reports or descriptions filled with details helps students meet the standards for writing. Students' oral presentation of ideas, questions, research findings, and experiences develops the students' listening and speaking skills.

The potential exists for GBE to support almost all of the English–language arts standards. Suggested student readings to supplement garden experiences are listed at the end of this publication.

Beyond the Core Academic Subjects

Many other areas of study beyond the core academic subjects can be enhanced by GBE; for example, in home economics students study consumer education, foods and nutrition, and health. Service-learning, agricultural literacy, environmental education, art, and music also lend themselves to GBE.

In service-learning, students fulfill community service requirements through garden-related projects, such as improving school lunches, beautifying the campus, feeding homeless people with produce from the garden, or providing nutrition education. In agricultural literacy programs, gardens provide teachers with an accessible, practical setting for their programs. In environmental education, gardens provide small-scale ecosystems that offer numerous opportunities for students to understand natural ecosystems. Gardens can provide inspiration for art and music projects and, in turn, art and music programs can enhance and expand on what children learn in the garden. For example, through drawing plants or learning songs with garden themes, children gain a new perspective on their garden experiences.

In the fall of 2000, East Palo Alto Charter School collaborated with Valley of the Hearts Delight and Hidden Villa. We transformed a former junkyard behind our classrooms into a flourishing, vibrant, organic garden.

Last year we started a service-learning project to make the garden easier for teachers, students, and families to use. The students involved in the project painted signs identifying plants in English and Spanish and covered the paths with mulch to clearly define them. They also organized the toolshed and developed a system to show what jobs needed to be done each week. They set up a compost system and made presentations to every class on how and why to compost.

At lunchtime the students monitored what their classmates put into the compost bins. Their efforts definitely made the garden easier to use and a more significant part of their classmates' education. By the end of the year, all grades, K–8, were composting and visiting the garden.

Sharon Johnson, Lead Teacher and Garden Coordinator
East Palo Alto Charter School
Ravenswood City School District
East Palo Alto

Food service is another important school garden partner. Some food service directors, concerned with students' diets, have begun collaborating with school garden programs to encourage students to eat more fresh fruits and vegetables. Students are more likely to taste and eat vegetables if they have grown vegetables in a school garden. Food service personnel and teachers at some schools are coordinating instruction for the classroom and the cafeteria around the history and nutritional value of particular crops. In addition, some food service directors are participating in farm-to-school programs. The directors purchase crops directly from nearby farms to bring the garden experience with fresh fruits and vegetables closer to the lunch experience in the school cafeteria.

The School Garden

Gardens are as different as the gardeners who develop and manage them and the schools in which they are found. There is no set of rules to follow to create a garden that encourages learning. Although sizes and shapes differ, school gardens are a place where students can have sensory experiences with the elements and organisms of the living world.

For the purposes of the guide, the minimum requirements for a school garden are as follows:

- A sunny space of any size and shape where children are able to grow, care for, or observe plants (Even an indoor space with

We, the cafeteria staff, have three raised beds that are ours in the school garden. We worked with the special day class on getting the ground ready. I thinned out my strawberries at home and had plenty for us to plant at school. Everything we grow goes into the weekly salad bar. The cafeteria staff and the kids work well together. Some of the food service staff come out during lunch break. I find the more the children see you do in the garden, the more they want to do.

Joanne Osburn
Food Service Director
Pixley Union School District
Pixley

ample natural light or appropriate artificial lighting may be suitable.)

- A source of water convenient to the space
- Students, teachers, and families (when possible) with the enthusiasm and dedication to make something new happen

Once the three requirements are met, teachers will find the following resources helpful:

- A plan or vision for the garden space
- Gardening tools and gloves
- School staff, families, or community members with gardening expertise
- Administrative support
- Teacher training in GBE
- Support from school grounds maintenance staff
- A compost pile
- Local sources of inexpensive garden supplies, such as tools, plants, and topsoil
- "Outdoor classroom" space where children can work comfortably at tables

Many of the activities listed in this guide involve plants grown for a particular activity. However, some activities may be done with plants commonly found in school yards, such as shade trees or lawn. Other activities are enhanced by certain perennial plants, such as those that attract insects or provide habitat for birds. Once planted and properly maintained, these plants can be available for years of use.

Garden development and management are large topics that are covered well in other publications; for example, *Children's Gardens; Digging Deeper; Getting Started; Farming Is Food, Fiber, Flowers . . . and Fun! A Workbook for Growers of School Gardens;* and *Sowing the Seeds of Success* (see Selected References at the end of this section). In addition, the California Department of Education offers free of charge a school garden resource packet, which includes *Getting Started,* along with many other useful resource materials and a list of Web sites.[1]

Gardening experts in the community are typically found in Master Gardener programs sponsored by the University of California Cooperative Extensions. These individuals often help establish school

[1] To order a packet, call the California Department of Education, Nutrition Services Division, at (916) 323-2473.

I spent my youth on a farm, an experience very few students have today. I want to make sure my students know where their food comes from, and I want them to know the taste of garden fresh vegetables and herbs. At the moment we are growing mustard greens, chard, chives, rosemary, parsley, sage, and nasturtiums; and we will use these in recipes we prepare in our industrial kitchen classroom.

Erevetta Marzette, Home Economics Careers and Technology Teacher
Dorsey High School
Los Angeles Unified School District
Los Angeles

Through their work in gardens, children are exposed to a learning experience that encourages consideration of the millions of species with which they share the planet's resources and an understanding of how human decisions affect wild communities. Absence of such experience leads to an inability to escape the constraints of human-centered thinking that ignores interdependencies and therefore impoverishes the human condition.

Gardens provide experiences that are the underpinnings of sustainable living, experiences of boundary, reach, and scale that engender a healthy self-limitation for the individual and the community. The little garden at the school is particularly critical to an education that makes these connections.

Janet Brown, Program Officer for Food Systems
Center for Ecoliteracy
Berkeley

gardens and have information on other resources, such as local garden clubs. Master Gardeners can be reached through the Cooperative Extension under county listings in the telephone directory. Contact information on the Master Gardener programs is also available on the Internet at <*www.mastergardeners.org*>. In addition, students in high school agricultural education programs and local college agriculture or horticulture programs often have significant knowledge and free time. Those students benefit from the opportunity to engage in community service through school garden management or direct instruction of elementary-age children.

Selected References

Alexander, J.; M. W. North; and D. K. Hendren. "Master Garden Classroom Garden Project: An Evaluation of the Benefits to Children," *Children's Environments,* Vol. 12 (1995), 256–63.

Bremner, E., and J. Pusey. *Children's Gardens: A Field Guide for Teachers, Parents and Volunteers.* Monterey Park: University of California Cooperative Extension Common Ground Garden Program, 1999.

Eames-Sheavly, M. *Sowing the Seeds of Success.* Burlington, Vt.: National Gardening Association, 1999.

Getting Started: A Guide for Creating School Gardens as Outdoor Classrooms. Berkeley: Center for Ecoliteracy and Life Lab Science Program, 1997. Available on request as part of the California Department of Education garden packet; call (916) 323-2473.

Kiefer, J., and M. Kemple. *Digging Deeper: Integrating Youth Gardens into Schools and Communities—A Comprehensive Guide.* Montpelier, Vt.: Common Roots Press and Food Works, 1998.

Lieberman, G. A., and L. L. Hoody. *Closing the Achievement Gap: Using the Environment as an Integrative Context for Learning.* Poway, Calif.: Science Wizards, 1998.

Morris, J.; M. Briggs; and S. Zidenberg-Cherr. "School-Based Gardens Can Teach Kids Healthier Eating Habits," *California Agriculture* (September/October 2000).

Sherbo, J. L. *Farming Is Food, Fiber, Flowers . . . and Fun! A Workbook for Growers of School Gardens.* Sacramento: The Agricultural Network, 2001.

Note: The publication data provided in this list were supplied by the Nutrition Services Division, California Department of Education. Questions about the materials should be addressed to that division at (916) 445-0850.

Grade Two

Many science and history–social science concepts can be taught in grade two through activities that take place in a school garden or through investigations that arise from the production of food in a garden. The science standards require students in grade two to study life cycles and plants' responses to the environment. Students look at rock, minerals, and soil and learn that soil is a resource. In history–social science they study the roles of people involved in the production and processing of food. Students look at land use in California and learn mapping skills. History is introduced by comparisons of "then" and "now" and a consideration of agricultural practices and food production.

In mathematics students add, subtract, multiply, measure with appropriate units, and collect and analyze data; those tasks can be embedded in school garden work. In English–language arts the curricular emphasis on reading means that second-grade students begin to extend their understanding of narrative and informational text and increase their overall proficiency in written and oral communication through assignments that relate to gardens and agriculture.

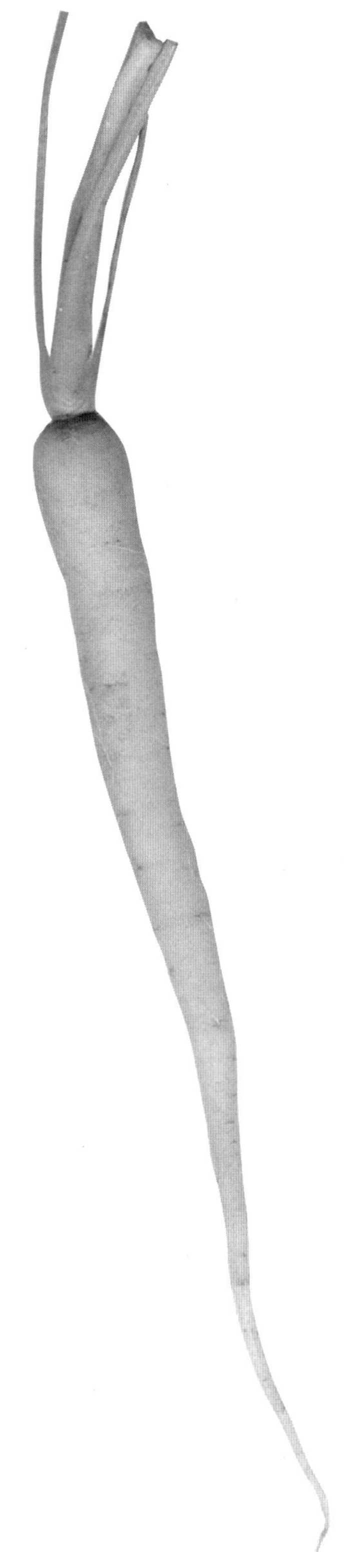

Few activities for mathematics and English–language arts are described in the garden-based teaching materials. However, the experienced teacher will not have difficulty in developing methods to expand the activities that are strong in science or social studies to include the use of mathematics and English–language arts skills. This process may be more difficult for less experienced teachers or teachers who are not familiar with a garden setting.

My second grade class and I started a garden in a small 10' x 10' square that was home to a tree. Many people tried to convince us of the uselessness of such an area. With the aid of some of our fathers, the Room One garden came into being.

We used the garden to discuss measurement. We measured the perimeter of the plot and the rows. As the garden began to grow, the students kept journals on the progress, describing the process of a plant growing from a seed.

We were successful enough to harvest on a weekly basis, and we shared vegetables with our school family. I used the garden to increase awareness of good eating habits, changing seasons, and responsibility. The children took pride and ownership in the garden area. They were protective of it. It gave parents and children something to discuss because it was visible to all as they used our campus.

The garden is a wonderful way to incorporate various standards with fun and interactive play, but it takes time and coordination.

Traci Thigpen, Teacher
Carver School
Compton Unified School District
Compton

Grade Two / Science

Table 2.1 Activities that support science standards

NOTE: To view the complete standards, go to <*www.cde.ca.gov/standards/*>.

	Standards		Gardening	Nutrition	Cooking	Waste mgmt.	Ag. systems	Instructional materials	Activities	Links to other grade 2 standards
			Content areas							
Physical Sciences	1. The motion of objects can be observed and measured. As a basis for understanding this concept:	d. Students know tools and machines are used to apply pushes and pulls (forces) to make things move.					•	*Simple and Complex Machines Used in Agriculture*	"Machines and People," p. 7: Students brainstorm about the definition of a machine and why people use machines. They study the tractor and think about machines at their homes.	SCI 1.c
							•	*Simple and Complex Machines Used in Agriculture*	"Six Kinds Do It All," p. 16: Students become familiar with six kinds of simple machines, learning how they function to help people work.	
Life Sciences	2. Plants and animals have predictable life cycles. As a basis for understanding this concept:	a. Students know that organisms reproduce offspring of their own kind and that the offspring resemble their parents and one another.	•		•			*TWIGS*	"Sprout Farmers," p. 113: Students grow several varieties of sprouts from seed and then compare and eat the sprouts.	SCI 2.c
			•					*TWIGS*	"Starting with Seeds," p. 15: Students explore different seed types, construct small greenhouses using zip-lock bags, and plant their seeds.	
						•		*Closing the Loop*	"Cycles in Nature and Red Worm Development," p. 135: Students observe and identify the stages of a red worm's life cycle. (This activity has a one-month preparation period.)	SCI 2.b, 4.f ELA W 2.1
		b. Students know the sequential stages of life cycles are different for different animals, such as butterflies, frogs, and mice.	•					*The Growing Classroom*	"The Butterfly Flutter By," p. 261: Students collect caterpillars and observe them until they become butterflies.	

Key: ELA—English–Language Arts; HSS—History–Social Science; L&S—Listening and Speaking; MATH—Mathematics; M&G—Measurement and Geometry; NS—Number Sense; R—Reading; SCI—Science; STATS—Statistics, Data Analysis, and Probability; W—Writing

Table 2.1 Activities that support science standards (Continued)

	Standards		Gardening	Nutrition	Cooking	Waste mgmt.	Ag. systems	Instructional materials	Activities	Links to other grade 2 standards
			Content areas							
Life Sciences	2. Plants and animals have predictable life cycles. As a basis for understanding this concept:	b. Students know the sequential stages of life cycles are different for different animals, such as butterflies, frogs, and mice.				•		*Closing the Loop*	"Cycles in Nature and Red Worm Development," p. 135: Students observe and identify the stages of a red worm's life cycle. (This activity has a one-month preparation period.)	SCI 2.a, 4.f ELA W 2.1
		c. Students know many characteristics of an organism are inherited from the parents. Some characteristics are caused or influenced by the environment.	•		•			*TWIGS*	"Sprout Farmers," p. 113: Students grow several varieties of sprouts from seed and then compare and eat the sprouts.	SCI 2.a
		e. Students know light, gravity, touch, or environmental stress can affect the germination, growth, and development of plants.	•					*The Growing Classroom*	"Seed to Earth, Seed to Earth, Do You Read Me?" p. 147: Students plant seeds in different soils and record the seeds' growth.	SCI 4.a
			•					*TWIGS*	"Seed Magic," p. 11: Students dissect seeds to examine their parts and then plant seeds with and without the conditions they need for growth, such as light, water, and good soil.	
			•					*The Growing Classroom*	"Room to Live," p. 145: Students discover the effects of planting density on seed growth.	SCI 4.a, 4.b
			•					*The Growing Classroom*	"Water We Doing?" p. 164: Students observe relationships between watering and plant growth.	SCI 4.b, MATH M&G 1.3
		f. Students know flowers and fruits are associated with reproduction in plants.	•					*Project Food, Land & People: Resources for Learning*	"Buzzy, Buzzy, Bee," p. 103: The class plays a pollination game in which bee players visit apple tree players. The result is a high number of apples from the trees.	

	Standards		Gardening	Nutrition	Cooking	Waste Mgmt.	Ag. Systems	Instructional materials	Activities	Links to other grade 2 standards
			Content areas							
Earth Sciences	3. Earth is made of materials that have distinct properties and provide resources for human activities. As a basis for understanding this concept:	a. Students know how to compare the physical properties of different kinds of rocks and know that rock is composed of different combinations of minerals.	•		•			*The Growing Classroom*	"Everyone Needs a Rock," p. 54: Students identify, explore, and classify rocks from the school yard.	
		b. Students know smaller rocks come from the breakage and weathering of larger rocks.	•				•	*The Growing Classroom*	"Space Travelers," p. 69: Students play alien space explorers who have come to Earth to study soil so that they will be able to manufacture it for their own planet.	SCI 3.c
		c. Students know that soil is made partly from weathered rock and partly from organic materials and that soils differ in their color, texture, capacity to retain water, and ability to support the growth of many kinds of plants.	•				•	*TWIGS*	"Soil," p. 6: Students examine soil samples to determine their content.	SCI 3.e
			•					*The Growing Classroom*	"So What? Sow Seeds!" p. 156: Students prepare soil mix for flats from different materials, learn what components make up a good soil and how soils may differ, and then sow the seeds in flats.	
			•				•	*The Growing Classroom*	"Space Travelers," p. 69: Students play alien space explorers who have come to Earth to study soil so that they will be able to manufacture it for their own planet.	SCI 3.b
			•				•	*The Growing Classroom*	"Water, Water Everywhere," p. 75: Students compare water-holding capacities of different soils and explain why the amounts of water differ.	

Key: ELA—English–Language Arts; HSS—History–Social Science; L&S—Listening and Speaking; MATH—Mathematics; M&G—Measurement and Geometry; NS—Number Sense; R—Reading; SCI—Science; STATS—Statistics, Data Analysis, and Probability; W—Writing

Table 2.1 Activities that support science standards (Continued)

Strand	Standards		Gardening	Nutrition	Cooking	Waste Mgmt.	Ag. Systems	Instructional materials	Activities	Links to other grade 2 standards
Earth Sciences	3. Earth is made of materials that have distinct properties and provide resources for human activities. As a basis for understanding this concept:	e. Students know rock, water, plants, and soil provide many resources, including food, fuel, and building materials, that humans use.					•	*Closing the Loop*	"What Are Natural Resources?" p. 5: Students learn about natural resources and the products people make from them. They identify natural resources on the school grounds and determine what resources were used to make various items.	ELA W 2.1
							•	*The Growing Classroom*	"Bioburgers," p. 110: Students make a food flowchart tracing all parts of a hamburger back to the source ingredients: sun, soil, water, and air.	
Investigation and Experimentation	4. Scientific progress is made by asking meaningful questions and conducting careful investigations. As a basis for understanding this concept and addressing the content in the other three strands, students should develop their own questions and perform investigations. Students will:	a. Make predictions based on observed patterns and not random guessing.	•					*The Growing Classroom*	"Seed to Earth, Seed to Earth, Do You Read Me?" p. 147: Students plant seeds in different soils and record the seeds' growth.	SCI 2.e
			•					*The Growing Classroom*	"Room to Live," p. 145: Students discover the effects of density on seed growth.	SCI 2.e, 4.b
			•		•			*Project Food, Land & People: Resources for Learning*	"We're into Pumpkins," p. 47: Students predict measurements of pumpkins, measure the pumpkins, record the data, then display the data on charts and bar graphs.	SCI 4.e MATH STATS 1.1, 1.2, 1.3, 1.4
		b. Measure length, weight, temperature, and liquid volume with appropriate tools and express those measurements in standard metric system units.	•					*The Growing Classroom*	"Room to Live," p. 145: Students discover the effects of planting density on seed growth.	SCI 2.e, 4.a
			•					*The Growing Classroom*	"Water We Doing?" p. 164: Students observe relationships between watering and plant growth.	SCI 2.e MATH M&G 1.3
			•					*The Growing Classroom*	"Temperature Hunt," p. 287: Students measure and record several different temperatures in the school yard or garden.	MATH STATS 1.1

	Standards	Gardening	Nutrition	Cooking	Waste mgmt.	Ag. systems	Instructional materials	Activities	Links to other grade 2 standards
		Content areas							
Investigation and Experimentation	c. Compare and sort common objects according to two or more physical attributes (e.g., color, shape, texture, size, weight).	•					*The Growing Classroom*	"Seedy Character," p. 112: Students observe, classify, and identify different kinds of seeds.	SCI 4.f ELA L&S 1.9
	d. Write or draw descriptions of a sequence of steps, events, and observations.	•					*The Growing Classroom*	"Room to Live," p. 145: While conducting an investigation, the teacher guides the students in drawing a sequence of their observations.	
	e. Construct bar graphs to record data, using appropriately labeled axes.	•					*Project Food, Land & People: Resources for Learning*	"We're into Pumpkins," p. 47: Students predict measurements of pumpkins, measure the pumpkins, record the data, then display the data on charts and bar graphs.	SCI 4.a MATH STATS 1.1, 1.2, 1.3, 1.4
	f. Use magnifiers or microscopes to observe and draw descriptions of small objects or small features of objects.	• •					*TWIGS* *The Growing Classroom*	"Pest or Pal?" p. 45: Students gather, investigate, and classify insects from the garden. "Seedy Character," p. 112: Students observe, classify, and identify different kinds of seeds.	SCI 4.c ELA L&S 1.9
	g. Follow oral instructions for a scientific investigation.	•					*The Growing Classroom*	"Water We Doing?" p. 164, or "Seed to Earth, Seed to Earth, Do You Read Me?" p. 147: The teacher uses only oral instruction to guide the students in conducting the investigation.	

Key: ELA—English–Language Arts; HSS—History–Social Science; L&S—Listening and Speaking; MATH—Mathematics; M&G—Measurement and Geometry; NS—Number Sense; R—Reading; SCI—Science; STATS—Statistics, Data Analysis, and Probability; W—Writing

Grade Two / History–Social Science

Table 3.2 Activities that support history–social science standards

NOTE: To view the complete standards, go to <*www.cde.ca.gov/standards/*>.

Standards		Content areas					Instructional materials	Activities	Links to other grade 2 standards
		Gardening	Nutrition	Cooking	Waste Mgmt.	Ag. Systems			
2.1 Students differentiate between things that happened long ago and things that happened yesterday.	1. Trace the history of a family through the use of primary and secondary sources, including artifacts, photographs, interviews, and documents.					•	An activity was not selected from the instructional materials. A general activity is suggested.	The teacher chooses a family involved in agriculture for several generations. Students learn about the family's immigration to California and the family's experience in farming before and after their arrival.	
	2. Compare and contrast their daily lives with those of their parents, grandparents, and/or guardians.					•	*Kids Cook Farm-Fresh Food*	"Dad's Ranch," p. 68: Students listen to the teacher read the profile of a California farmer. It explores changes in farm management and the daily life of that farmer and his sons over the farmer's lifetime.	
2.2 Students demonstrate map skills by describing the absolute and relative locations of people, places, and environments.	1. Locate on a simple letter-number grid system the specific locations and geographic features in their neighborhood or community (e.g., map of the classroom, the school).	•				•	An activity was not selected from the instructional materials. A general activity is suggested.	Students include public gardens, community gardens, and farms, along with other neighborhood features, on the map.	
2.4 Students understand basic economic concepts and their individual roles in the economy and demonstrate basic economic reasoning skills.	1. Describe food production and consumption long ago and today, including the roles of farmers, processors, distributors, weather, and land and water resources.					•	*Project Food, Land & People: Resources for Learning*	"Tomatoes to Ketchup, Chickens to Omelettes," p. 39: Students learn about the connections between raw and processed foods and explore the steps through which a crop goes to become the finished product.	

Standards		Gardening	Nutrition	Cooking	Waste mgmt.	Ag. systems	Instructional materials	Activities	Links to other grade 2 standards
		Content areas							
	2. Understand the role and interdependence of buyers (consumers) and sellers (producers) of goods and services.	•				•	*Kids Cook Farm-Fresh Food*	"A School Produce Stand," p. 66: Students sell produce to fellow students.	MATH NS 5.1, 5.2
	3. Understand how limits on resources affect production and consumption (what to produce and what to consume).					•	*Project Food, Land & People: Resources for Learning*	"Don't Use It All Up!" p. 57: Students participate in a demonstration using sponges and water to show how people consume finite resources.	SCI 4.d
2.5 Students understand the importance of individual action and character and explain how heroes from long ago and the recent past have made a difference in others' lives (e.g., from biographies of Abraham Lincoln, Louis Pasteur, Sitting Bull, George Washington Carver, Marie Curie, Albert Einstein, Golda Meir, Jackie Robinson, Sally Ride).						•	An activity was not selected from the instructional materials. A general activity is suggested.	Students study the life and work of a hero, such as César Chávez or George Washington Carver.	

Key: ELA—English–Language Arts; HSS—History–Social Science; L&S—Listening and Speaking; MATH—Mathematics; M&G—Measurement and Geometry; NS—Number Sense; R—Reading; SCI—Science; STATS—Statistics, Data Analysis, and Probability; W—Writing

Grade Two / Mathematics

Table 2.3 Activities that support mathematics standards

NOTE: To view the complete standards, go to <*www.cde.ca.gov/standards/*>.

	Standards		Gardening	Nutrition	Cooking	Waste Mgmt.	Ag. Systems	Instructional materials	Activities	Links to other grade 2 standards
			Content areas							
Number Sense	5.0 Students model and solve problems by representing, adding, and subtracting amounts of money:	5.1 Solve problems using combinations of coins and bills.	•				•	*Kids Cook Farm-Fresh Food*	"A School Produce Stand," p. 66: Students sell produce to fellow students. They carry out all monetary transactions with purchasers at the stand.	HSS 2.4.2 MATH NS 5.2
		5.2 Know and use the decimal notation and the dollar and cent symbols for money.	•				•	*Kids Cook Farm-Fresh Food*	"A School Produce Stand," p. 66: Students sell produce to fellow students. They carry out all monetary transactions with purchasers at the stand.	HSS 2.4.2 MATH NS 5.1
Measurement and Geometry	1.0 Students understand that measurement is accomplished by identifying a unit of measure, iterating (repeating) that unit, and comparing it to the item to be measured:	1.3 Measure the length of an object to the nearest inch and/or centimeter.				•		*Worms Eat Our Garbage*	"Sizing Up Cocoons," p. 17: Students measure the length and height of drawings of worm cocoons using millimeters and centimeters.	
			•					*The Growing Classroom*	"Water We Doing?" p. 164: Students observe relationships between watering and plant growth.	SCI 2.e, 4.b

Statistics, Data Analysis, and Probability

Standards		Gardening	Nutrition	Cooking	Waste Mgmt.	Ag. Systems	Instructional materials	Activities	Links to other grade 2 standards
1.0 Students collect numerical data and record, organize, display, and interpret the data on bar graphs and other representations:	1.1 Record numerical data in systematic ways, keeping track of what has been counted.	•		•			*Project Food, Land & People: Resources for Learning*	"We're into Pumpkins," p. 47: Students predict measurements of pumpkins, measure the pumpkins, record the data, then display the data on charts and bar graphs.	SCI 4.a, 4.e MATH STATS 1.2, 1.3, 1.4
		•					*The Growing Classroom*	"Temperature Hunt," p. 287: Students measure and record several different temperatures in the school yard or garden.	SCI 4.b
	1.2 Represent the same data set in more than one way (e.g., bar graphs and charts with tallies).	•		•			*Project Food, Land & People: Resources for Learning*	"We're into Pumpkins," p. 47: Students predict measurements of pumpkins, measure the pumpkins, record the data, then display the data on charts and bar graphs.	SCI 4.a, 4.e MATH STATS 1.1, 1.3, 1.4
	1.3 Identify features of data sets (range and mode).	•		•			*Project Food, Land & People: Resources for Learning*	"We're into Pumpkins," p. 47: Students predict measurements of pumpkins, measure the pumpkins, record the data, then display the data on charts and bar graphs.	SCI 4.a, 4.e MATH STATS 1.1, 1.2, 1.4
	1.4 Ask and answer simple questions related to data representations.	•		•			*Project Food, Land & People: Resources for Learning*	"We're into Pumpkins," p. 47: Students predict measurements of pumpkins, measure the pumpkins, record the data, then display the data on charts and bar graphs.	SCI 4.a, 4.e MATH STATS 1.1, 1.2, 1.3

Key: ELA—English–Language Arts; HSS—History–Social Science; L&S—Listening and Speaking; MATH—Mathematics; M&G—Measurement and Geometry; NS—Number Sense; R—Reading; SCI—Science; STATS—Statistics, Data Analysis, and Probability; W—Writing

Grade Two / English–Language Arts

Table 2.4 Activities that support English–language arts standards

NOTE: To view the complete standards, go to <*www.cde.ca.gov/standards/*>.

	Standards		Gardening	Nutrition	Cooking	Waste Mgmt.	Ag. Systems	Instructional materials	Activities	Links to other grade 2 standards
Reading	2.0 Reading Comprehension	*Structural Features of Informational Materials* 2.1 Use titles, tables of contents, and chapter headings to locate information in expository text.	•					*TWIGS*	"You Are the Expert," p. 3: Students use expository texts, such as reference materials, magazines, and pamphlets, to research a gardening topic and then report their findings back to the group.	ELA L&S 1.9, 2.2
Writing	2.0 Writing Applications (Genres and Their Characteristics)	2.1 Write brief narratives based on their experiences: a. Move through a logical sequence of events. b. Describe the setting, characters, objects, and events in detail.				•		*Closing the Loop*	"Cycles in Nature and Red Worm Development," p. 135: Students observe and identify the stages of a red worm's life cycle and then describe what they have learned in several ways, including writing a story and composing a poem. (This activity has a one-month preparation period.)	SCI 2.a, 2.b, 4.f
Listening and Speaking	1.0 Listening and Speaking Strategies	*Comprehension* 1.1 Determine the purpose or purposes of listening (e.g., to obtain information, to solve problems, for enjoyment).	•				•	*The Growing Classroom*	"10-4 Good Buddy," p. 25: Students play a communication game that teaches listening skills within the context of a group discussion about what they like to learn in science.	ELA L&S 1.2, 1.3
		Comprehension 1.2 Ask for clarification and explanation of stories and ideas.	•				•	*The Growing Classroom*	"10-4 Good Buddy," p. 25: Students play a communication game that teaches listening skills within the context of a group discussion about what they like to learn in science.	ELA L&S 1.1, 1.3
		Comprehension 1.3 Paraphrase information that has been shared orally by others.	•				•	*The Growing Classroom*	"10-4 Good Buddy," p. 25: Students play a communication game that teaches listening skills within the context of a group discussion about what they like to learn in the garden.	ELA L&S 1.1, 1.2

	Standards		Gardening	Nutrition	Cooking	Waste Mgmt.	Ag. Systems	Instructional materials	Activities	Links to other grade 2 standards
			Content areas							
Listening and Speaking		*Organization and Delivery of Oral Communication* 1.5 Organize presentations to maintain a clear focus.					•	*Closing the Loop*	"Treasures of the Earth—A Play," p. 43: Students perform a play about the importance of natural resources and pledge to conserve them.	ELA L&S 1.6
		Organization and Delivery of Oral Communication 1.6 Speak clearly and at an appropriate pace for the type of communication (e.g., informal discussion, report to class).					•	*Closing the Loop*	"Treasures of the Earth—A Play," p. 43: Students perform a play about the importance of natural resources and pledge to conserve them.	ELA L&S 1.5
		Organization and Delivery of Oral Communication 1.9 Report on a topic with supportive facts and details.	•					*TWIGS*	"You Are the Expert," p. 3: Students use expository texts, such as reference materials, magazines, and pamphlets, to research a gardening topic and then report their findings back to the group.	ELA R 2.1; L&S 2.2
			•					*The Growing Classroom*	"Seedy Character," p. 112: Students observe, classify, and identify different kinds of seeds. Students share their classification schemes.	SCI 4.c, 4.f
	2.0 Speaking Applications (Genres and Their Characteristics)	2.2 Report on a topic with facts and details, drawing from several sources of information.	•					*TWIGS*	"You Are the Expert," p. 3: Students use expository texts, such as reference materials, magazines, and pamphlets, to research a gardening topic and then report their findings back to the group.	ELA R 2.1; L&S 1.9

Key: ELA—English–Language Arts; HSS—History–Social Science; L&S—Listening and Speaking; MATH—Mathematics; M&G—Measurement and Geometry; NS—Number Sense; R—Reading; SCI—Science; STATS—Statistics, Data Analysis, and Probability; W—Writing

Grade Three

The science standards for grade three are designed to introduce students to fundamental patterns in nature and to the means by which students understand the world around them. Garden-based education is particularly appropriate for teaching the position of the sun in the sky through the day and during the seasons. Students learn that energy comes from the sun and is stored in food and that the adaptations in living organisms' structure or behavior allow different organisms to survive in different environments.

In history–social science students in grade three study continuity and change in their local region. Because agriculture is an important part of the economy in most regions of California, students can investigate California food systems and compare them to school garden food production. Garden-based education is well adapted to the teaching of the physical and cultural geography of California regions.

To meet mathematics standards in the third grade, students estimate, measure, describe, and classify objects. Students are introduced to fractions, primarily through concrete objects and diagrams. Science standards may be integrated with mathematics standards by

emphasizing repeated observations and using patterns to help solve problems. Garden-based activities can readily support these standards although few of the current materials meet this potential.

In English–language arts students in grade three are taught to write descriptions that use concrete sensory details to present unified impressions of people, places, things, or experiences. Students are required to learn speaking strategies and share prose, poetry, personal narratives, and experiences with fluency and expression. Gardens are the setting for many experiences that students may draw on in writing and speaking. Students can also read fairy tales or myths centered on gardens and food to progress in achieving the language arts standards for this grade level. Literature about American Indian agriculture and food systems connects gardens to both the English–language arts and the history–social science standards for the third grade.

As I gaze at our school garden here in Union City, I remember the landscape of 30 years ago. The Greenleaf Wholesale Nursery raised carnations and roses in commercial greenhouses that lined up in neat rows much like the rows of flowers inside. The nursery belonged to the Kitayama family, who were longtime residents, local business people, and community leaders. Our school is named for Tom Kitayama, who was mayor of Union City for a quarter of a century and who cultivated the nursery business. As the city grew in size, the nursery was moved, and the landscape changed into housing and now hosts our elementary school.

As a third grade teacher, I teach from the state history–social science standards, imparting to the students an understanding of their local community and communicating the concept of "then and now." Through a partnership with the Kitayama family and local businesses and organizations, we added a greenhouse to our garden. What better way to teach students about their community and those who served it than to rebuild a part of what had come before?

We have come full circle at Kitayama Elementary, learning of our past heritage and adding to our present in a way that will leave memories with our students that will carry them into the future.

Cherie Barnecut, Teacher
Tom Kitayama Elementary School
New Haven Unified School District
Union City

Grade Three / Science

Table 3.1 Activities that support science standards

NOTE: To view the complete standards, go to <*www.cde.ca.gov/standards/*>.

	Standards		Gardening	Nutrition	Cooking	Waste Mgmt.	Ag. Systems	Instructional materials	Activities	Links to other grade 3 standards
			Content areas							
Physical Sciences	1. Energy and matter have multiple forms and can be changed from one form to another. As a basis for understanding this concept:	a. Students know energy comes from the Sun to Earth in the form of light.	•					*Junior Master Gardener*	"Money Trees," p. 119: Students visit a shaded site and a sunny site around a building on a sunny day to understand that trees influence the amount of solar energy reaching a building.	SCI 2.a
			•					*The Growing Classroom*	"We've Got Solar Power!" p. 305: Students design and construct simple miniature solar collectors.	
		b. Students know sources of stored energy take many forms, such as food, fuel, and batteries.		•				*The Growing Classroom*	"Burn Out," p. 356: The teacher burns various foods to demonstrate that energy is stored in food and that food provides energy for the body.	SCI 1.c
		c. Students know machines and living things convert stored energy to motion and heat.		•				*The Growing Classroom*	"Burn Out," p. 356: The teacher burns various foods to demonstrate that energy is stored in food and that food provides energy for the body.	SCI 1.b
		e. Students know matter has three forms: solid, liquid, and gas.	•					An activity was not selected from the instructional materials. A general activity is suggested.	Students look in the garden and identify, where found, a liquid, a solid, and a gas.	
		f. Students know evaporation and melting are changes that occur when the objects are heated.	•					*The Growing Classroom*	"Plant Sweat," p. 135: Students conduct an experiment with potted plants to demonstrate transpiration of water.	SCI 5.a, 5.d, 5.e

	Standards		Gardening	Nutrition	Cooking	Waste mgmt.	Ag. systems	Instructional materials	Activities	Links to other grade 3 standards
			Content areas							
Physical Sciences	2. Light has a source and travels in a direction. As a basis for understanding this concept:	a. Students know sunlight can be blocked to create shadows.	•					*Junior Master Gardener*	"Money Trees," p. 119: Students visit a shaded site and a sunny site around a building on a sunny day to understand that trees influence the amount of energy reaching a building.	SCI 1.a
		b. Students know light is reflected from mirrors and other surfaces.	•					*The Growing Classroom*	"Star Food," p. 143: Students use foil to reflect light onto some of the plants in a garden. They compare the rates of growth between the plants that receive light and those that do not.	SCI 5.c
Life Sciences	3. Adaptations in physical structure or behavior may improve an organism's chance for survival. As a basis for understanding this concept:	a. Students know plants and animals have structures that serve different functions in growth, survival, and reproduction.	•					*Junior Master Gardener*	"Flower Dissection," p. 11: Each student dissects a flower.	
			•					*The Growing Classroom*	"Let's Get a Handle on This," p. 128: Students conduct an experiment with climbing peas to observe the plants' use of tendrils.	SCI 5.e MATH M&G 1.1
			•					*The Growing Classroom*	"Adapt a Seed," p. 118: Students use classroom materials to design imaginary seeds to show various dispersal mechanisms, such as floating, attracting animals, and hitchhiking.	
			•					*Project Food, Land & People: Resources for Learning*	"Investigating Insects," p. 181: Students observe insects in the school environment and identify and label body parts.	
						•		*Closing the Loop*	"Getting to Know Red Worms," p. 121: Students study red worms and answer questions about the worms' anatomy.	

Key: ELA—English–Language Arts; HSS—History–Social Science; L&S—Listening and Speaking; MATH—Mathematics; M&G—Measurement and Geometry; MR—Mathematical Reasoning; NS—Number Sense; R—Reading; SCI—Science; W—Writing

Table 3.1 Activities that support science standards (Continued)

	Standards		Gardening	Nutrition	Cooking	Waste Mgmt.	Ag. Systems	Instructional materials	Activities	Links to other grade 3 standards
Life Sciences	3. Adaptations in physical structure or behavior may improve an organism's chance for survival. As a basis for understanding this concept:	b. Students know examples of diverse life forms in different environments, such as oceans, deserts, tundra, forests, grasslands, and wetlands.				•		*Worms Eat Our Garbage*	"No Worms Here," p. 34: Students answer questions on environments in which they would find earthworms.	
		c. Students know living things cause changes in the environment in which they live: some of these changes are detrimental to the organism or other organisms, and some are beneficial.	•					*Junior Master Gardener*	"Power Seeds," p. 16: Students observe the force that seeds exhibit during germination.	SCI 3.a, 5.d
			•					*The Growing Classroom*	"The Great and Powerful Earthworm," p. 279: Students investigate earthworms as soil tillers.	SCI 5.d
			•					*The Growing Classroom*	"Natural Defense," p. 249: Students conduct an experiment in weed growth by using leaves from certain plants to demonstrate how a plant can emit natural poisons that inhibit the growth of neighboring plants.	
			•					*TWIGS*	"Rotation," p. 37: Students play a simulation game demonstrating the use of nutrients by different plants and the need for crop rotation.	SCI 3.d
			•					*Closing the Loop*	"The Effects Worms Have on Soil," p. 143: Students examine worm castings and discuss how the activities of worms affect soil.	
		d. Students know when the environment changes, some plants and animals survive and reproduce; others die or move to new locations.	•					*TWIGS*	"Rotation," p. 37: Students play a simulation game demonstrating the use of nutrients by different plants and the need for crop rotation.	SCI 3.c
						•		*Worms Eat Our Garbage*	"Warm/Cold Adaptation," p. 26: Students answer questions about how worms respond to variations in temperature.	ELA R 2.3

	Standards		Content areas: Gardening	Nutrition	Cooking	Waste Mgmt.	Ag. Systems	Instructional materials	Activities	Links to other grade 3 standards
Life Sciences			•					*The Growing Classroom*	"To Dig or Not to Dig," p. 81: Students study the effects of soil compaction on plant growth.	SCI 5.c, 5.d, 5.e
Earth Sciences	4. Objects in the sky move in regular and predictable patterns. As a basis for understanding this concept:	e. Students know the position of the Sun in the sky changes during the course of the day and from season to season.	•					*Junior Master Gardener*	"The Zones," p. 152: Students study a climate map, locating their community and identifying appropriate plants for the different zones. They then go outside to note the position of the sun in the sky during the day in relation to north, south, east, and west.	SCI 3.b HSS 3.1.2
Investigation and Experimentation	5. Scientific progress is made by asking meaningful questions and conducting careful investigations. As a basis for understanding this concept and addressing the content in the other three strands, students should develop their own questions and perform investigations. Students will:	a. Repeat observations to improve accuracy and know that the results of similar scientific investigations seldom turn out exactly the same because of differences in the things being investigated, methods being used, or uncertainty in the observation.	•					*The Growing Classroom*	"Plant Sweat," p. 135: Students conduct an experiment with potted plants to demonstrate transpiration of water.	SCI 1.f, 5.d, 5.e

Key: ELA—English–Language Arts; HSS—History–Social Science; L&S—Listening and Speaking; MATH—Mathematics; M&G—Measurement and Geometry; MR—Mathematical Reasoning; NS—Number Sense; R—Reading; SCI—Science; W—Writing

Table 3.1 Activities that support science standards (Continued)

	Standards		Gardening	Nutrition	Cooking	Waste Mgmt.	Ag. Systems	Instructional materials	Activities	Links to other grade 3 standards
			Content areas							
Investigation and Experimentation	5. Scientific progress is made by asking meaningful questions and conducting careful investigations. As a basis for understanding this concept and addressing the content in the other three strands, students should develop their own questions and perform investigations. Students will:	b. Differentiate evidence from opinion and know that scientists do not rely on claims or conclusions unless they are backed by observations that can be confirmed.	•					*Junior Master Gardener*	"What's Not the Same," p. 12: Students test the influence of light on plant growth.	SCI 5.d, 5.e
			•					*Junior Master Gardener*	"More Mulch, More Moist," p. 136: Students evaluate how the use of mulch affects water conservation.	SCI 5.c, 5.e MATH M&G 1.1
						•		*Worms Eat Our Garbage*	"Is That a Fact?" p. 50: Students differentiate fact from opinion.	
			•					*The Growing Classroom*	"Sugar Factories," p. 132: The teacher reads a short story to the class about a historical science experiment that examined how plants grow. Students discuss the opinions of other scientists who performed similar experiments and answer questions about the conclusions of the experiment described in the story.	ELA L&S 1.1, 1.3
		c. Use numerical data in describing and comparing objects, events, and measurements.	•					*Junior Master Gardener*	"More Mulch, More Moist," p. 136: Students evaluate how the use of mulch affects water conservation.	SCI 5.b, 5.e MATH M&G 1.1
			•					*Project Food, Land & People: Resources for Learning*	"We're into Pumpkins," p. 47: Students measure pumpkins in different ways and investigate their origin.	MATH M&G 1.1; MR 2.1
			•					*The Growing Classroom*	"What Good Is Compost?" p. 91: Students grow two identical crops, one in a bed with compost and one in a bed without compost. They take data on the rate at which either growth or germination occurs.	SCI 5.e

	Standards	Gardening	Nutrition	Cooking	Waste mgmt.	Ag. systems	Instructional materials	Activities	Links to other grade 3 standards
Investigation and Experimentation	d. Predict the outcome of a simple investigation and compare the result with the prediction.	•					*Junior Master Gardener*	"What's Not the Same," p. 12: Students test the influence of light on plant growth.	SCI 5.b, 5.e
		•					*The Growing Classroom*	"Plant Sweat," p. 135: Students conduct an experiment with potted plants to demonstrate transpiration of water. They make predictions and compare their predictions to the result of the experiment.	SCI 1.f, 5.a, 5.e
	e. Collect data in an investigation and analyze those data to develop a logical conclusion.	•					*Junior Master Gardener*	"What's Not the Same," p. 12: Students test the influence of light on plant growth.	SCI 5.b, 5.d
		•					*Junior Master Gardener*	"More Mulch, More Moist," p. 136: Students evaluate how the use of mulch affects water conservation.	SCI 5.b, 5.c MATH M&G 1.1
		•					*The Growing Classroom*	"Plant Sweat," p. 135: Students conduct an experiment with potted plants to demonstrate transpiration of water. They collect and analyze data.	SCI 1.f, 5.a, 5.d
		•					*The Growing Classroom*	"What Good Is Compost?" p. 91: Students grow two identical crops, one in a bed with compost and one in a bed without compost. They take data on the rate at which either growth or germination occurs.	SCI 5.c

Key: ELA—English–Language Arts; HSS—History–Social Science; L&S—Listening and Speaking; MATH—Mathematics; M&G—Measurement and Geometry; MR—Mathematical Reasoning; NS—Number Sense; R—Reading; SCI—Science; W—Writing

Grade Three / History–Social Science

Table 3.2 Activities that support history–social science standards

NOTE: To view the complete standards, go to <*www.cde.ca.gov/standards/*>.

Standards		Gardening	Nutrition	Cooking	Waste Mgmt.	Ag. Systems	Instructional materials	Activities	Links to other grade 3 standards
3.1 Students describe the physical and human geography and use maps, tables, graphs, photographs, and charts to organize information about people, places, and environments in a spatial context.	1. Identify geographical features in their local region (e.g., deserts, mountains, valleys, hills, coastal areas, oceans, lakes).	•				•	An activity was not selected from the instructional materials. A general activity is suggested.	Students identify geographical features in their region and use this information to make choices about what crops to plant in the school garden.	
	2. Trace the ways in which people have used the resources of the local region and modified the physical environment (e.g., a dam constructed upstream changed a river or coastline).	•					*Junior Master Gardener*	"The Zones," p. 152: Students study a climate map, locating their community and identifying appropriate plants for the different zones. They then go outside to note the position of the sun in the sky during the day in relation to north, south, east, and west.	SCI 3.b, 4.e
						•	*Kids Cook Farm-Fresh Food*	"Cities and Farms," p. 194: Students consider the opportunities and challenges for a family farm in an increasingly urban area.	ELA R 2.6
						•	*Project Food, Land & People: Resources for Learning*	"Don't Use It All Up," p. 57: Students explore water use and conservation by demonstrating how sponges and water symbolize human resource consumption.	

Standards		Content areas: Gardening	Nutrition	Cooking	Waste mgmt.	Ag. systems	Instructional materials	Activities	Links to other grade 3 standards
3.2 Students describe the American Indian nations in their local region long ago and in the recent past.	1. Describe national identities, religious beliefs, customs, and various folklore traditions.	•				•	An activity was not selected from the instructional materials. A general activity is suggested.	Students read stories about important American Indian foods. They grow the plants described in those stories in their school garden.	
	2. Discuss the ways in which physical geography, including climate, influenced how the local Indian nations adapted to their natural environment (e.g., how they obtained food, clothing, tools).	•				•	An activity was not selected from the instructional materials. A general activity is suggested.	Students research important American Indian foods and grow them in the school garden. Students identify the tools the Indians used and compare them with those the students use in the school garden.	
	4. Discuss the interaction of new settlers with the already established Indians of the region.					•	An activity was not selected from the instructional materials. A general activity is suggested.	Students investigate the role of food and medicinal plants in the interactions between the Indians and settlers.	
3.3 Students draw from historical and community resources to organize the sequence of local historical events and describe how each period of settlement left its mark on the land.	1. Research the explorers who visited here, the newcomers who settled here, and the people who continue to come to the region, including their cultural and religious traditions and contributions.			•			*Project Food, Land & People: Resources for Learning*	"Gala Fiesta Jamboree," p. 169: Students explore the role of harvest festivals in diverse cultures and within their local community.	

Key: ELA—English–Language Arts; HSS—History–Social Science; L&S—Listening and Speaking; MATH—Mathematics; M&G—Measurement and Geometry; MR—Mathematical Reasoning; NS—Number Sense; R—Reading; SCI—Science; W—Writing

Table 3.2 Activities that support history–social science standards (Continued)

Standards		Content areas: Gardening	Nutrition	Cooking	Waste Mgmt.	Ag. Systems	Instructional materials	Activities	Links to other grade 3 standards
3.3 Students draw from historical and community resources to organize the sequence of local historical events and describe how each period of settlement left its mark on the land.	2. Describe the economies established by settlers and their influence on the present-day economy, with emphasis on the importance of private property and entrepreneurship.					•	An activity was not selected from the instructional materials. A general activity is suggested.	Students describe the role of local agriculture and food production in the economy of the settlers.	
	3. Trace why their community was established, how individuals and families contributed to its founding and development, and how the community has changed over time, drawing on maps, photographs, oral histories, letters, newspapers, and other primary sources.					•	An activity was not selected from the instructional materials. A general activity is suggested.	Students do research on the role of agriculture in community development in California and discuss urban pressures on agriculture.	
3.5 Students demonstrate basic economic reasoning skills and an understanding of the economy of the local region.	1. Describe the ways in which local producers have used and are using natural resources, human resources, and capital resources to produce goods and services in the past and the present.					•	*Simple and Complex Machines Used in Agriculture*	"Machines in Agriculture," p. 51: Students learn that simple and complex machines increase the efficiency of producing food and other agricultural crops.	ELA W 2.2

Standards		Content areas					Instructional materials	Activities	Links to other grade 3 standards
		Gardening	Nutrition	Cooking	Waste Mgmt.	Ag. Systems			
	2. Understand that some goods are made locally, some elsewhere in the United States, and some abroad.					•	*The Growing Classroom*	"Lunch Bag Ecology, Part Two," p. 220: Students analyze how their lunch was transported, stored, and prepared.	
			•				*Junior Master Gardener*	"Dr. Fruit," p. 141: Students research the origins and relevant information about fruits and nuts.	ELA R 2.6
						•	*The Growing Classroom*	"This Little Lettuce Went to Market," p. 378: Students investigate and compare the roads to market for local produce and for produce grown far away.	
	4. Discuss the relationship of students' "work" in school and their personal human capital.					•	*Junior Master Gardener*	"Careers and School," p. 211: Students discuss the ways in which school is like the world of work and draw a card that lists a career, including careers in the food system. They are then asked to list one or more school subjects relating to that career.	

Key: ELA—English–Language Arts; HSS—History–Social Science; L&S—Listening and Speaking; MATH—Mathematics; M&G—Measurement and Geometry; MR—Mathematical Reasoning; NS—Number Sense; R—Reading; SCI—Science; W—Writing

Grade Three / Mathematics

Table 3.3 Activities that support mathematics standards

NOTE: To view the complete standards, go to <*www.cde.ca.gov/standards/*>.

	Standards		Content areas: Gardening	Nutrition	Cooking	Waste Mgmt.	Ag. Systems	Instructional materials	Activities	Links to other grade 3 standards
Number Sense	3.0 Students understand the relationship between whole numbers, simple fractions, and decimals:	3.2 Add and subtract simple fractions (e.g., determine that $\frac{1}{8} + \frac{3}{8}$ is the same as $\frac{1}{2}$).			•			*Junior Master Gardener*	"Garden Veggie Casserole," p. 178: Students bake a casserole with vegetables and answer questions about fractions of teaspoons and tablespoons.	
Algebra and Functions	1.0 Students select appropriate symbols, operations, and properties to represent, describe, simplify, and solve simple number relationships:	1.4 Express simple unit conversions in symbolic form (e.g., __ inches = __ feet × 12).					•	*Junior Master Gardener*	"A Bushel and a Peck," p. 144: Students are introduced to units of volume used in the food system and are asked to convert between them.	
Measurement and Geometry	1.0 Students choose and use appropriate units and measurement tools to quantify the properties of objects:	1.1 Choose the appropriate tools and units (metric and U.S.) and estimate and measure the length, liquid volume, and weight/mass of given objects.			•			*Kids Cook Farm-Fresh Food*	Recipes: The teacher selects a crop that reflects local agricultural production. Students then follow a recipe for that crop.	ELA R 2.7
			•					*Junior Master Gardener*	"Site Map," p. 121: Students use mathematics skills to generate a landscape design.	
			•					*Junior Master Gardener*	"More Mulch, More Moist," p.136: Students evaluate how the use of mulch affects water conservation.	SCI 5.b, 5.c, 5.e

	Standards	Content areas					Instructional materials	Activities	Links to other grade 3 standards
		Gardening	Nutrition	Cooking	Waste mgmt.	Ag. systems			
Measurement and Geometry	1.2 Estimate or determine the area and volume of solid figures by covering them with squares or by counting the number of cubes that would fill them.	•					*Junior Master Gardener*	"Small and Large," p. 160: Students measure the garden area and determine appropriate spacing for seeds.	MATH M&G 1.3
					•		*Worms Eat Our Garbage*	"How Big a Bin?" p. 70: Students determine the volume of various shapes of worm bins and answer questions about appropriately sized bins.	

Key: ELA—English–Language Arts; HSS—History–Social Science; L&S—Listening and Speaking; MATH—Mathematics; M&G—Measurement and Geometry; MR—Mathematical Reasoning; NS—Number Sense; R—Reading; SCI—Science; W—Writing

Grade Three / English–Language Arts

Table 3.4 Activities that support English–language arts standards

NOTE: To view the complete standards, go to <*www.cde.ca.gov/standards/*>.

	Standards		Content areas					Instructional materials	Activities	Links to other grade 3 standards
			Gardening	Nutrition	Cooking	Waste Mgmt.	Ag. Systems			
Reading	2.0 Reading Comprehension	*Structural Features of Informational Materials* 2.1 Use titles, tables of contents, chapter headings, glossaries, and indexes to locate information in text.	•					*The Growing Classroom*	"Zip Code Seeds," p. 116: Students choose seeds from catalogs on the basis of suitable climate, food preference, and aesthetic appeal.	MATH NS 3.3
		Comprehension and Analysis of Grade-Level-Appropriate Text 2.2 Ask questions and support answers by connecting prior knowledge with literal information found in, and inferred from, the text.			•			*Junior Master Gardener*	"Johnny's Appleslop," p. 149: The teacher (or a student) reads aloud a story about Johnny Appleseed. Students answer questions and make applesauce.	
		Comprehension and Analysis of Grade-Level-Appropriate Text 2.3 Demonstrate comprehension by identifying answers in the text.				•		*Worms Eat Our Garbage*	"Worm Body Quiz," p. 2: Students answer questions about the anatomy of worms.	
		Comprehension and Analysis of Grade-Level-Appropriate Text 2.7 Follow simple multiple-step written instructions (e.g., how to assemble a product or play a board game).			•			*Kids Cook Farm-Fresh Food*	Recipes: The teacher selects a crop that reflects local agricultural production. Students then follow a recipe for that crop.	MATH M&G 1.1
					•			*TWIGS*	"Apples," p. 82: Students make and eat a snack made from apples after discussing and observing different varieties.	

	Standards		Gardening	Nutrition	Cooking	Waste mgmt.	Ag. systems	Instructional materials	Activities	Links to other grade 3 standards
			Content areas							
Reading	3.0 Literary Response and Analysis	*Narrative Analysis of Grade-Level-Appropriate Text* 3.3 Determine what characters are like by what they say or do and by how the author or illustrator portrays them.				•		*Closing the Loop*	"Using Compost and Promoting Vermicomposting," p. 149: Students read or listen to stories about Miss Rumphius and Johnny Appleseed and discuss the specific things each character did to improve the environment.	
Writing	1.0 Writing Strategies	*Organization and Focus* 1.1 Create a single paragraph: a. Develop a topic sentence. b. Include simple supporting facts and details.				•		*Worms Eat Our Garbage*	"My Worm Story," p. 19: Students listen to a story starter and write a story about their experiences with worms.	
						•		*Junior Master Gardener*	"Compost Sandwich Composition," p. 33: Students write a paragraph to support the claim that preparing compost is important.	
	2.0 Writing Applications (Genres and Their Characteristics)	2.2 Write descriptions that use concrete sensory details to present and support unified impressions of people, places, things, or experiences.	•					*The Growing Classroom*	"Little Munchkins," p. 59: Students work in pairs outdoors to record their observations as they pretend they are miniature people on a 100-inch hike.	

Key: ELA—English–Language Arts; HSS—History–Social Science; L&S—Listening and Speaking; MATH—Mathematics; M&G—Measurement and Geometry; MR—Mathematical Reasoning; NS—Number Sense; R—Reading; SCI—Science; W—Writing

Table 3.4 Activities that support English–language arts standards (Continued)

	Standards		Gardening	Nutrition	Cooking	Waste Mgmt.	Ag. Systems	Instructional materials	Activities	Links to other grade 3 standards
Listening and Speaking	1.0 Listening and Speaking Strategies	*Comprehension* 1.1 Retell, paraphrase, and explain what has been said by a speaker.	•					*Junior Master Gardener*	"Coconut Float," p. 13: Students read a poem about seed dispersal.	SCI 3.a
		Comprehension 1.3 Respond to questions with appropriate elaboration.	•					*The Growing Classroom*	"Lotus Seeds," p. 122: Students listen to a story about lotus seeds and then answer questions.	SCI 3.a
		Organization and Delivery of Oral Communication 1.9 Read prose and poetry aloud with fluency, rhythm, and pace, using appropriate intonation and vocal patterns to emphasize important passages of the text being read.	• •					*Junior Master Gardener* *Junior Master Gardener*	"Plant Parts Rap," p. 8: Students read aloud a poem on plant parts. "A Fruit's Life Rhyme," p. 151: Students read a rhyme that describes the life cycle of plants.	
	2.0 Speaking Applications (Genres and Their Characteristics)	2.3 Make descriptive presentations that use concrete sensory details to set forth and support unified impressions of people, places, things, or experiences.				•		*Closing the Loop*	"The Basics of Vermicomposting," p. 107: Students learn about recycling food scraps and compose a poem about vermicomposting.	MATH M&G 1.1

Grade Four

Garden-based education supports the science standards for grade four, particularly the life sciences standards, extremely well. Students learn that plants are the primary source of matter and energy entering most food chains, that producers and consumers are related through food chains and food webs and may compete with each other for resources in an ecosystem, and that many insects and microorganisms are beneficial. Students learn how to characterize ecosystems, and they study the interdependence of living organisms in an ecosystem. Most of the teaching materials reviewed for this guide include activities that support the science standards at this grade level.

The focus of the history–social science standards in grade four is on California. Students learn the story of their state and study its physical

Gardens Are the Perfect Teaching Tools

for motivation of
different styles of learning
continuity of skill acquisition
personal discoveries of texture-odor-taste
propagating respect for the tenacity and fragility of plants
from countless ever-changing details
building a conceptional picture
framing the "Natural Order"
of Earth's ecosystems

Holiday Matchett, Teacher
Birch Lane School
Davis Joint Unified School District
Davis

and human geography, including the influence of immigration on the state. Students gain knowledge of how California became an agricultural power.

The mathematics standards require students in grade four to understand addition, subtraction, multiplication, and division of multidigit whole numbers. Students collect, represent, and analyze data to answer questions and communicate their findings to others. The teaching materials included in *A Child's Garden of Standards* offer a variety of mathematics activities at this level.

At the fourth grade the English–language arts standards emphasize, for the first time, reading to learn rather than learning to read. Standards on research and technology call for students to explore a variety of print materials, including almanacs, newspapers, and periodicals, and electronic reference materials. Students in grade four write narratives, informational reports, and summaries and make oral presentations. Garden-based education provides exciting subjects for students to read and to write reports on and present their results. Numerous activities are listed for English–language arts standards. In addition, teachers can integrate the English–language arts standards on research with the science standards on ecosystems.

Grade Four / Science

Table 4.1 Activities that support science standards

NOTE: To view the complete standards, go to <*www.cde.ca.gov/standards/*>.

	Standards		Gardening	Nutrition	Cooking	Waste Mgmt.	Ag. Systems	Instructional materials	Activities	Links to other grade 4 standards
Life Sciences	2. All organisms need energy and matter to live and grow. As a basis for understanding this concept:	a. Students know plants are the primary source of matter and energy entering most food chains.	•					*The Growing Classroom*	"I Eat the Sun," p. 213: Students receive labels representing the sun, plants, microorganisms, snails, chickens, and coyotes. Wearing labels, students organize themselves into a food chain to show how energy and nutrients move through the chain.	
			•					*Project Food, Land & People: Resources for Learning*	"Gifts from the Sun," p. 203: Students play-act the basics of photosynthesis.	
				•				*Nutrition to Grow On*	"Introduction to Nutrition and Gardening," p. 9, Nutrition Activities: Students trace the source of popular foods back to plants.	ELA L&S 1.1
		b. Students know producers and consumers (herbivores, carnivores, omnivores, and decomposers) are related in food chains and food webs and may compete with each other for resources in an ecosystem.				•		*Junior Master Gardener*	"Composting Critter Page," p. 33: Students study the organisms found in a worm bin.	
						•		*Worms Eat Our Garbage*	"Who Am I?" p. 87: Students play a guessing game to identify animals found in a worm bin and learn how these animals are related in food chains and food webs.	ELA R 1.1
						•		*Worms Eat Our Garbage*	"Food Web of the Compost Pile," p. 89: Students study a diagram of the food web of a compost pile and answer questions about the diagram.	

Key: ELA—English–Language Arts; HSS—History–Social Science; L&S—Listening and Speaking; MATH—Mathematics; MR—Mathematics Reasoning; NS—Number Sense; R—Reading; SCI—Science; STATS—Statistics, Data Analysis, and Probability; W—Writing

Table 4.1 Activities that support science standards (Continued)

	Standards		Gardening	Nutrition	Cooking	Waste Mgmt.	Ag. Systems	Instructional materials	Activities	Links to other grade 4 standards
Life Sciences	2. All organisms need energy and matter to live and grow. As a basis for understanding this concept:	c. Students know decomposers, including many fungi, insects, and microorganisms, recycle matter from dead plants and animals.				•		*Closing the Loop*	"The Nutrient Cycle and Other Cycles," p. 451: Students observe the life cycle of trees and the decomposition of leaves, then read stories on the topic.	SCI 6.c ELA L&S 1.2; R 2.3, 2.5; W 1.1
						•		*Closing the Loop*	"Scavengers and Decomposers," p. 459: Students study scavengers and see examples of the actions of decomposers.	SCI 6.c, 6.d
			•			•		*Nutrition to Grow On*	"Nutrients We Need," p. 27, Gardening Activity: Students make a worm composting system in a bottle and observe the process of decomposition.	
						•		*The Growing Classroom*	"You Are What You Eat," p. 217: Students are assigned the roles of different animals or plants. Then they use string to connect themselves with other animals in the food web.	
						•		*The Growing Classroom*	"Compost Bags," p. 194: Students manage natural decomposition by creating a compost system in a bag.	
	3. Living organisms depend on one another and on their environment for survival. As a basis for understanding this concept:	a. Students know ecosystems can be characterized by their living and nonliving components.				•		*Project Food, Land & People: Resources for Learning*	"From Apple Cores to Healthy Soil," p. 111: Students conduct a composting experiment that reveals how soil organisms, temperature, air, and water can decompose organic matter and enrich soil.	SCI 2.c, 6.c
			•					*Kids Cook Farm-Fresh Food*	"Finding the Right Soil for Your Plant," p. 56: Students perform two soil experiments to observe the drainage and settling qualities of different soils.	

	Standards	Gardening	Nutrition	Cooking	Waste mgmt.	Ag. systems	Instructional materials	Activities	Links to other grade 4 standards
Life Sciences	b. Students know that in any particular environment, some kinds of plants and animals survive well, some survive less well, and some cannot survive at all.					•	*Project Food, Land & People: Resources for Learning*	"Amazing Grazing," p. 441: Students in groups receive scenarios describing various environments. Each group determines human needs and the ability of the group's assigned environment to meet those needs.	ELA L&S 1.5
		•					*The Growing Classroom*	"What's to Worry?" p. 96: Students design and test ways to protect plants from frost damage.	SCI 6.c, 6.d, 6.e
		•			•		*The Growing Classroom*	"What Good Is Compost?" p. 91: Students grow two identical crops, one in a bed with compost and one in a bed without compost.	SCI 6.b, 6.c, 6.e MATH STATS 1.3
		•					*Junior Master Gardener*	"It's a Small World," p. 88: Students make a Berlese funnel and use it to collect and observe insects from different garden habitats.	
	c. Students know many plants depend on animals for pollination and seed dispersal, and animals depend on plants for food and shelter.	•					*Nutrition to Grow On*	"Consumerism," p. 127, Gardening Activity: Students look at plant adaptations for attracting pollinators, then make colorful butterfly models.	
		•					*Project Food, Land & People: Resources for Learning*	"Buzzy, Buzzy Bee," p. 103: Students pretend to be honey bees and apple trees, then graph the number of apples produced after pollination.	MATH STATS 1.3

Key: ELA—English–Language Arts; HSS—History–Social Science; L&S—Listening and Speaking; MATH—Mathematics; MR—Mathematics Reasoning; NS—Number Sense; R—Reading; SCI—Science; STATS—Statistics, Data Analysis, and Probability; W—Writing

Table 4.1 Activities that support science standards (Continued)

	Standards		Content areas					Instructional materials	Activities	Links to other grade 4 standards
			Gardening	Nutrition	Cooking	Waste Mgmt.	Ag. Systems			
Life Sciences	3. Living organisms depend on one another and on their environment for survival. As a basis for understanding this concept:	c. Students know many plants depend on animals for pollination and seed dispersal, and animals depend on plants for food and shelter.	•					*Junior Master Gardener*	"The Bartering System," p. 99: Students play a game of exchanging energy for pollination services to learn how plants and insects trade services.	
			•					*Kids Cook Farm-Fresh Food*	"Seed Saving and Sowing," p. 22: Students perform an activity in which they determine which tomato seeds are viable. They learn about the role of animals in the spreading of seeds.	
		d. Students know that most microorganisms do not cause disease and that many are beneficial.	•					*The Growing Classroom*	"The Matchmaker, Part Two," p. 93: Students examine nitrogen-fixing nodules on the roots of legume cover crops.	
Earth Sciences	5. Waves, wind, water, and ice shape and reshape Earth's land surface. As a basis for understanding this concept:	b. Students know natural processes, including freezing and thawing and the growth of roots, cause rocks to break down into smaller pieces.	•					An activity was not selected from the instructional materials. A general activity is suggested.	Students look for evidence of roots breaking rocks, concrete, or asphalt in the garden or on the school grounds.	

	Standards		Gardening	Nutrition	Cooking	Waste mgmt.	Ag. systems	Instructional materials	Activities	Links to other grade 4 standards
			Content areas							
Earth Sciences		c. Students know moving water erodes landforms, reshaping the land by taking it away from some places and depositing it as pebbles, sand, silt, and mud in other places (weathering, transport, and deposition).	•					*The Growing Classroom*	"Splash," p. 99: Students study rain and soil erosion.	SCI 6.d, 6.f
			•				•	*Project Food, Land & People: Resources for Learning*	"Till We or Won't We?" p. 213: Students simulate rain on a field to investigate how soil preparation, tillage, and mulch affect soil erosion and water runoff.	SCI 5.a, 6.c, 6.d, 6.f
Investigation and Experimentation	6. Scientific progress is made by asking meaningful questions and by conducting careful investigations. As a basis for understanding this concept and addressing the content in the other three strands, students should develop their own questions and perform investigations. Students will:	a. Differentiate observation from inference (interpretation) and know scientists' explanations come partly from what they observe and partly from how they interpret their observations.	•					*The Growing Classroom*	"Sugar Factories," p. 132: Students listen to a short story read by the instructor that describes a historical science experiment. They discuss what the results of the experiment told the scientist about how plants grow.	SCI 2.a ELA L&S 1.1, 1.2
		b. Measure and estimate the weight, length, or volume of objects.				•		*Closing the Loop*	"Performing a Class Audit of Waste," p. 321: Students evaluate and record the waste stream over a period of days, then calculate percentages and compare types of waste.	ELA L&S 1.1, 1.2
			•			•		*The Growing Classroom*	"What Good Is Compost?" p. 91: Students grow two identical crops, one in a bed with compost and one in a bed without compost, then graph and compare their findings.	SCI 3.b, 6.c, 6.e MATH STATS 1.3

Key: ELA—English–Language Arts; HSS—History–Social Science; L&S—Listening and Speaking; MATH—Mathematics; MR—Mathematics Reasoning; NS—Number Sense; R—Reading; SCI—Science; STATS—Statistics, Data Analysis, and Probability; W—Writing

Table 4.1 Activities that support science standards (Continued)

Strand	Standards		Gardening	Nutrition	Cooking	Waste Mgmt.	Ag. Systems	Instructional materials	Activities	Links to other grade 4 standards
Investigation and Experimentation	6. Scientific progress is made by asking meaningful questions and by conducting careful investigations. As a basis for understanding this concept and addressing the content in the other three strands, students should develop their own questions and perform investigations. Students will:	c. Formulate and justify predictions based on cause-and-effect relationships.				•		*Closing the Loop*	"What Decomposes?" p. 475: Students bury several objects to test them for their tendency to decompose.	SCI 6.d, 6.f ELA W 2.1
			•			•		*Closing the Loop*	"What Is Composting and Why Is It Important?" p. 481: Students conduct experiments to identify the five essential components in the production of compost.	SCI 2.c, 6.d, 6.f ELA W 2.1
					•			*TWIGS*	"Safe and Clean," p. 65: Students discuss the value of hand washing and test the growth of bacteria on bread handled before and after the students have washed their hands.	
			•					*Nutrition to Grow On*	"Introduction to Nutrition and Gardening," p. 9, Gardening Activity: Students test plant growth by using varying amounts of water and light.	
			•			•	•	*Kids Cook Farm-Fresh Food*	"Making Compost 'Tea,'" p. 78: Students make compost "tea" and conduct an experiment to measure its effect on plant growth.	SCI 6.b
			•					*The Growing Classroom*	"What's to Worry?" p. 96: Students design and test ways of protecting plants from frost damage.	SCI 3.b, 6.d, 6.e
			•			•		*The Growing Classroom*	"What Good Is Compost?" p. 91: Students grow two identical crops, one in a bed with compost and one in a bed without compost.	SCI 3.b, 6.b, 6.e

Strand	Standards	Gardening	Nutrition	Cooking	Waste Mgmt.	Ag. Systems	Instructional materials	Activities	Links to other grade 4 standards
		Content areas							
Investigation and Experimentation	d. Conduct multiple trials to test a prediction and draw conclusions about the relationships between predictions and results.				•		*Closing the Loop*	"What Decomposes?" p. 475: Students bury several objects to test them for their tendency to decompose.	SCI 6.c ELA W 2.1
		•			•		*Closing the Loop*	"What Is Composting and Why Is It Important?" p. 481: Students conduct experiments to identify the five essential components in the production of compost.	SCI 2.c, 6.c, 6.f ELA W 2.1
		•					*The Growing Classroom*	"What's to Worry?" p. 96: Students design and test ways of protecting plants from frost damage.	SCI 3.b, 6.c, 6.e
	e. Construct and interpret graphs from measurements.	•					*Nutrition to Grow On*	"The Food Guide Pyramid," p. 43, Gardening Activity: Students chart the growth of plants.	
		•			•		*The Growing Classroom*	"What Good Is Compost?" p. 91: Students grow two identical crops, one in a bed with compost and one in a bed without compost, then graph and compare their findings.	SCI 3.b, 6.b, 6.c MATH STATS 1.3
		•					*The Growing Classroom*	"What's to Worry?" p. 96: Students design and test ways of protecting plants from frost damage. They graph their findings.	SCI 3.b, 6.c, 6.d
	f. Follow a set of written instructions for a scientific investigation.	•			•		*Closing the Loop*	"What Is Composting and Why Is It Important?" p. 481: Students conduct experiments to identify the five essential components in the production of compost.	SCI 2.c, 6.c, 6.d ELA W 2.1

Key: ELA—English–Language Arts; HSS—History–Social Science; L&S—Listening and Speaking; MATH—Mathematics; MR—Mathematics Reasoning; NS—Number Sense; R—Reading; SCI—Science; STATS—Statistics, Data Analysis, and Probability; W—Writing

Grade Four / History–Social Science

Table 4.2 Activities that support history–social science standards

NOTE: To view the complete standards, go to <*www.cde.ca.gov/standards/*>.

Standards		Gardening	Nutrition	Cooking	Waste mgmt.	Ag. systems	Instructional materials	Activities	Links to other grade 4 standards
4.1 Students demonstrate an understanding of the physical and human geographic features that define places and regions in California.	1. Explain and use the coordinate grid system of latitude and longitude to determine the absolute locations of places in California and on Earth.	•					An activity was not selected from the instructional materials. A general activity is suggested.	Students determine the latitude and longitude of the school and school garden.	
	2. Distinguish between the North and South Poles; the equator and the prime meridian; the tropics; and the hemispheres, using coordinates to plot locations.	•				•	*Junior Master Gardener*	"The Zones," p. 152: Students discuss maps and globes and identify the poles and the equator. They also discuss appropriate plants and crops for different zones.	
	3. Identify the state capital and describe the various regions of California, including how their characteristics and physical environments (e.g., water, landforms, vegetation, climate) affect human activity.					•	*Fruits and Vegetables for Health*	"California Crops: From the Farm to the Table," p. 15: Students place production of various commodities on a map of California, research the commodities, and report to the class on their findings.	ELA W 2.3; L&S 2.2

Standards		Content areas: Gardening	Nutrition	Cooking	Waste mgmt.	Ag. systems	Instructional materials	Activities	Links to other grade 4 standards
4.2 Students describe the social, political, cultural, and economic life and interactions among people of California from the pre-Columbian societies to the Spanish mission and Mexican rancho periods.	1. Discuss the major nations of California Indians, including their geographic distribution, economic activities, legends, and religious beliefs; and describe how they depended on, adapted to, and modified the physical environment by cultivation of land and use of sea resources.					•	An activity was not selected from the instructional materials. A general activity is suggested.	Students investigate the diets of local American Indians and study oak trees and the processing of acorns for human consumption.	
		•				•		Students plant an American Indian garden and read folklore about corn and other important crops.	
		•				•		Students grow California native plants and investigate the early use of irrigation.	
	5. Describe the daily lives of the people, native and non-native, who occupied the presidios, missions, ranchos, and pueblos.	•				•	An activity was not selected from the instructional materials. A general activity is suggested.	Students plant a mission garden.	HSS 4.2.6
	6. Discuss the role of the Franciscans in changing the economy of California from a hunter-gatherer economy to an agricultural economy.	•				•	An activity was not selected from the instructional materials. A general activity is suggested.	Students plant a mission garden.	HSS 4.2.5
	8. Discuss the period of Mexican rule in California and its attributes, including land grants, secularization of the missions, and the rise of the rancho economy.					•	An activity was not selected from the instructional materials. A general activity is suggested.	Students investigate the history of ranching in Mexico and California.	

Key: ELA—English–Language Arts; HSS—History–Social Science; L&S—Listening and Speaking; MATH—Mathematics; MR—Mathematics Reasoning; NS—Number Sense; R—Reading; SCI—Science; STATS—Statistics, Data Analysis, and Probability; W—Writing

Table 4.2 Activities that support history–social science standards (Continued)

Standards		Content areas					Instructional materials	Activities	Links to other grade 4 standards
		Gardening	Nutrition	Cooking	Waste mgmt.	Ag. systems			
4.3 Students explain the economic, social, and political life in California from the establishment of the Bear Flag Republic through the Mexican-American War, the Gold Rush, and the granting of statehood.	3. Analyze the effects of the Gold Rush on settlements, daily life, politics, and the physical environment (e.g., using biographies of John Sutter, Mariano Guadalupe Vallejo, Louise Clapp).					•	An activity was not selected from the instructional materials. A general activity is suggested.	Students investigate the introduction of new foods to California during the Gold Rush.	
4.4 Students explain how California became an agricultural and industrial power, tracing the transformation of the California economy and its political and cultural development since the 1850s.	4. Describe rapid American immigration, internal migration, settlement, and the growth of towns and cities (e.g., Los Angeles).					•	An activity was not selected from the instructional materials. A general activity is suggested.	Students study the roles of immigration and migration on agriculture and the growth of towns and cities.	
	5. Discuss the effects of the Great Depression, the Dust Bowl, and World War II on California.					•	An activity was not selected from the instructional materials. A general activity is suggested.	Students investigate how California agriculture was affected by the Dust Bowl and the Great Depression. They read *The Gardener,* by Sarah Stewart.	ELA R 3.2, 3.3

Grade Four / Mathematics

Table 4.3 Activities that support mathematics standards

NOTE: To view the complete standards, go to <*www.cde.ca.gov/standards/*>.

	Standards		Gardening	Nutrition	Cooking	Waste Mgmt.	Ag. Systems	Instructional materials	Activities	Links to other grade 4 standards
Number Sense	1.0 Students understand the place value of whole numbers and decimals to two decimal places and how whole numbers and decimals relate to simple fractions. Students use the concepts of negative numbers:	1.7 Write the fraction represented by a drawing of parts of a figure; represent a given fraction by using drawings; and relate a fraction to a simple decimal on a number line.	•					*Junior Master Gardener*	"Paper Towel Gardening," p. 165: Students fold paper towels to represent fractions of the whole, then they place one seed per section according to the plant's space requirements.	
Number Sense	3.0 Students solve problems involving addition, subtraction, multiplication, and division of whole numbers and understand the relationships among the operations:	3.1 Demonstrate an understanding of, and the ability to use, standard algorithms for the addition and subtraction of multidigit numbers.	•					*Kids Cook Farm-Fresh Food*	"A School Produce Stand," p. 66: Students sell produce from the garden and use standard algorithms for the addition and subtraction of multidigit numbers.	MATH NS 3.2; MR 2.6
Number Sense		3.3 Solve problems involving multiplication of multidigit numbers by two-digit numbers.				•		*Worms Eat Our Garbage*	"Worm City Story," p. 152: Students read a paragraph and then solve problems related to the number of worms, how much they eat, and how much money the town saves on garbage collection by using worms to eat garbage.	

Key: ELA—English–Language Arts; HSS—History–Social Science; L&S—Listening and Speaking; MATH—Mathematics; MR—Mathematics Reasoning; NS—Number Sense; R—Reading; SCI—Science; STATS—Statistics, Data Analysis, and Probability; W—Writing

Table 4.3 Activities that support mathematics standards (Continued)

	Standards		Content areas: Gardening	Nutrition	Cooking	Waste Mgmt.	Ag. Systems	Instructional materials	Activities	Links to other grade 4 standards
Measurement and Geometry	1.0 Students understand perimeter and area:	1.1 Measure the area of rectangular shapes by using appropriate units, such as square centimeter (cm^2), square meter (m^2), square kilometer (km^2), square inch (in^2), square yard (yd^2), or square mile (mi^2).				•		*Worms Eat Our Garbage*	"How Big a Bin?" p. 70: Students measure worm bins of different sizes, then answer questions on the bins as worm habitats.	
Statistics, Data Analysis, and Probability	1.0 Students organize, represent, and interpret numerical and categorical data and clearly communicate their findings:	1.1 Formulate survey questions; systematically collect and represent data on a number line; and coordinate graphs, tables, and charts.		•				*Project Food, Land & People: Resources for Learning*	"Why I Buy," p. 517: Groups of students conduct a consumer preference trial. After collecting, graphing, and analyzing the data, students decide which brand of a product they will purchase and why.	
							•	*Project Food, Land & People: Resources for Learning*	"It All Starts with A," p. 273: Students conduct surveys to learn how agriculture provides for people. Students organize, simplify, and communicate their findings by using tallies, frequency tables, and histograms.	MATH STATS 1.3
					•		•	*Kids Cook Farm-Fresh*	"Frozen, Canned, or Fresh: Which Do You Prefer?" p. 88: Students survey student preferences for frozen, canned, and fresh spinach. They collect and graph data and communicate their findings to the class.	MATH STATS 1.3
				•				*Nutrition to Grow On*	"Goal Setting," p. 113, Nutrition Activities: Students chart the number of personal nutrition goals they meet over a four-day period and interpret the data.	ELA L&S 1.1

	Standards		Gardening	Nutrition	Cooking	Waste mgmt.	Ag. systems	Instructional materials	Activities	Links to other grade 4 standards
Statistics, Data Analysis, and Probability		1.3 Interpret one- and two-variable data graphs to answer questions about a situation.	•			•		*The Growing Classroom*	"What Good Is Compost?" p. 91: Students grow two identical crops, one in a bed with compost and one in a bed without compost, then graph and compare their findings.	SCI 3.b, 6.b, 6.c, 6.e
						•		*Worms Eat Our Garbage*	"Worm Population Growth," p. 109: Students study the growth of worms in various soil samples, then answer questions.	SCI 3.b
						•		*Worms Eat Our Garbage*	"Fox Sandy Loam," p. 106: Students study a graph and chart, then answer questions related to the topic.	
Mathematical Reasoning	2.0 Students use strategies, skills, and concepts in finding solutions:	2.3 Use a variety of methods, such as words, numbers, symbols, charts, graphs, tables, diagrams, and models, to explain mathematical reasoning.	•					*Junior Master Gardener*	"Small and Large," p. 160: Students consider space requirements for plants by pretending to be plants and verbally describing their needs, mapping an area on the floor, and plotting a garden bed on graph paper.	

Key: ELA—English–Language Arts; HSS—History–Social Science; L&S—Listening and Speaking; MATH—Mathematics; MR—Mathematics Reasoning; NS—Number Sense; R—Reading; SCI—Science; STATS—Statistics, Data Analysis, and Probability; W—Writing

Grade Four / English–Language Arts

Table 4.4 Activities that support English–language arts standards

NOTE: To view the complete standards, go to <*www.cde.ca.gov/standards/*>.

	Standards		Gardening	Nutrition	Cooking	Waste mgmt.	Ag. systems	Instructional materials	Activities	Links to other grade 4 standards
Reading	1.0 Word Analysis, Fluency and Systematic Vocabulary Development	*Word Recognition* 1.1 Read narrative and expository text aloud with grade-appropriate pacing, intonation, and expression.					•	*Kids Cook Farm-Fresh Food*	Crop descriptions and farm profiles: Students read selections that include facts about various California farming regions, farming methods, and environmental characteristics, such as climate and soil.	
		Vocabulary and Concept Development 1.3 Use knowledge of root words to determine the meaning of unknown words within a passage.				•		*Worms Eat Our Garbage*	"Classic Names," p. 8, and "More Classic Names," p. 10: Students use the English meanings of Latin or Greek words to analyze the meanings of scientific terms and the names of worm species.	
		Vocabulary and Concept Development 1.5 Use a thesaurus to determine related words and concepts.					•	*Project Food, Land & People: Resources for Learning*	"Expression Connection," p. 159: Students in groups play a word game that builds on the connections between farming, food, land, and people.	
	2.0 Reading Comprehension	*Comprehension and Analysis of Grade-Level-Appropriate Text* 2.4 Evaluate new information and hypotheses by testing them against known information and ideas.	•					*Kids Cook Farm-Fresh Food*	"Uncovering Cover Crops," p. 174, and "Heath Family Farm," p. 176: Students read about cover crops and explore one benefit of cover cropping by conducting an experiment. Students then draw their own conclusions.	

	Standards		Gardening	Nutrition	Cooking	Waste mgmt.	Ag. systems	Instructional materials	Activities	Links to other grade 4 standards
			Content areas							
Reading	3.0 Literary Response and Analysis	*Narrative Analysis of Grade-Level-Appropriate Text* 3.3 Use knowledge of the situation and setting and of a character's traits and motivations to determine the causes for that character's actions.	•		•			*Junior Master Gardener*	"Johnny's Appleslop," p. 149: Students listen to (or read aloud) a story about Johnny Appleseed. They answers questions about the story, then make applesauce.	
Writing	1.0 Writing Strategies	*Organization and Focus* 1.1 Select a focus, an organizational structure, and a point of view based upon purpose, audience, length, and format requirements.				•		*Closing the Loop*	"Promo and Play on Composting," p. 493: Students complete a writing project to make others aware of the importance of composting. Or they write, rehearse, and perform a play to encourage composting.	ELA W 1.10
		Evaluation and Revision 1.10 Edit and revise selected drafts to improve coherence and progression by adding, deleting, consolidating, and rearranging text.				•		*Closing the Loop*	"Promo and Play on Composting," p. 493: Students complete a writing project to make others aware of the importance of composting. Or they write, rehearse, and perform a play to encourage composting.	ELA W 1.1

Key: ELA—English–Language Arts; HSS—History–Social Science; L&S—Listening and Speaking; MATH—Mathematics; MR—Mathematics Reasoning; NS—Number Sense; R—Reading; SCI—Science; STATS—Statistics, Data Analysis, and Probability; W—Writing

Table 4.4 Activities that support English–language arts standards (Continued)

	Standards		Gardening	Nutrition	Cooking	Waste mgmt.	Ag. systems	Instructional materials	Activities	Links to other grade 4 standards
Writing	2.0 Writing Applications (Genres and Their Characteristics)	2.3 Write information reports: a. Frame a central question about an issue or situation. b. Include facts and details for focus. c. Draw from more than one source of information (e.g., speakers, books, newspapers, other media sources).					•	*Fruits and Vegetables for Health*	"California Crops: From the Farm to the Table," p. 15: Students place production of various commodities on a map of California, research the commodities, and report to the class on their findings.	HSS 4.1.3 ELA L&S 2.2
		2.4 Write summaries that contain the main ideas of the reading selection and the most significant details.					•	*Kids Cook Farm-Fresh Food*	Students read a farm profile from one or more chapters, then describe the main idea and supporting details in journals.	
Listening and Speaking	1.0 Listening and Speaking Strategies	*Comprehension* 1.1 Ask thoughtful questions and respond to relevant questions with appropriate elaboration in oral settings.	•					*The Growing Classroom*	"Sugar Factories," p. 132: Students listen to a short story read by the instructor that describes a historical science experiment. They discuss what the results of the experiment told the scientist about how plants grow.	SCI 2.a, 6.a ELA L&S 1.2
				•				*Nutrition to Grow On*	"Food Labels," p. 79, Nutrition Activities: Students learn how to read food labels and discuss the nutritional value of eight foods.	

	Standards		Gardening	Nutrition	Cooking	Waste mgmt.	Ag. systems	Instructional materials	Activities	Links to other grade 4 standards
Listening and Speaking		*Comprehension* 1.3 Identify how language usages (e.g., sayings, expressions) reflect regions and cultures.	•					*The Growing Classroom*	"The Power of the Circle," p. 175: Students are introduced to the concept of circles and to cycles found in nature. They learn about the importance of cycles to American Indian culture as described in a short essay read aloud to them.	
		Comprehension 1.4 Give precise directions and instructions.	•					*Junior Master Gardener*	"Plant a Seed," p. 199: Students in pairs engage in an activity in which one student verbally directs another student to plant a seed but gives no visual clues.	
		Analysis and Evaluation of Oral Media Communication 1.10 Evaluate the role of the media in focusing attention on events and in forming opinions on issues.		•				*Nutrition to Grow On*	"Consumerism," p. 127, Nutrition Activities: Students study the role of advertising in influencing consumers' food choices.	ELA L&S 1.1
	2.0 Speaking Applications (Genres and Their Characteristics)	2.1 Make narrative presentations: a. Relate ideas, observations, or recollections about an event or experience. b. Provide a context that enables the listener to imagine the circumstances of the event or experience. c. Provide insight into why the selected event or experience is memorable.		•				*Kids Cook Farm-Fresh Food*	Recipes: After preparing recipes and eating the food, students share observations, preferences, and insights.	

Key: ELA—English–Language Arts; HSS—History–Social Science; L&S—Listening and Speaking; MATH—Mathematics; MR—Mathematics Reasoning; NS—Number Sense; R—Reading; SCI—Science; STATS—Statistics, Data Analysis, and Probability; W—Writing

Grade Five

To meet science standards students in grade five study plant structure, respiration, digestion, waste disposal, and transportation of material in plants. Students plan and conduct experiments and gather and analyze data.

History–social science in the fifth grade focuses on the development of the United States through 1850, with an emphasis on the changing population. Students learn how people obtained food and how agriculture changed over time. Students also study trade routes, migration patterns, folklore, and political and economic forces that shaped the United States.

In mathematics the students increase their facility with the four basic arithmetic operations as applied to fractions, decimals, and percents. Students learn to measure angles, and they work with formulas to determine the area and the volume of objects. They collect, display, and analyze data by looking at the mean, median, and mode.

English–language arts standards require students in grade five to read aloud expository and narrative texts, especially informational material. Students write multiple-paragraph narrative and expository compositions and develop research skills. The GBE materials provide reading material for students with reading and writing opportunities that support other subject-area standards. The selection of appropriate garden-based literature allows additional standards to be addressed.

I had the good fortune of visiting the McGrath family farm in Camarillo recently with a busload of urban Los Angeles fifth graders. The group was very excited about our excursion out into the fields to see many different crops growing. The children delighted in picking and eating the sun-warmed strawberries! We all enjoyed sampling raw, freshly harvested corn.

It is important for urban children and their families to visit farms to better understand and appreciate the origins of the food they eat. There is something very wonderful about walking out into a field, smelling the soil and the plants, talking to the farm workers who tend the crops, and pulling one's own carrot out of the soil.

Nonnie Korten, Project Director
The Partnership for Agriculture and Science in Education
Los Angeles Unified School District
Los Angeles

Grade Five / Science

Table 5.1 Activities that support science standards

NOTE: To view the complete standards, go to <*www.cde.ca.gov/standards/*>.

	Standards		Gardening	Nutrition	Cooking	Waste Mgmt.	Ag. Systems	Instructional materials	Activities	Links to other grade 5 standards
Physical Sciences	1. Elements and their combinations account for all the varied types of matter in the world. As a basis for understanding this concept:	f. Students know differences in chemical and physical properties of substances are used to separate mixtures and identify compounds.	•					*The Growing Classroom*	"The Nitty-Gritty," p. 73: Students separate soil according to the physical properties of its three major components: sand, silt, and clay.	SCI 6.a
Life Sciences	2. Plants and animals have structures for respiration, digestion, waste disposal, and transport of materials. As a basis for understanding this concept:	a. Students know many multicellular organisms have specialized structures to support the transport of materials.	•	•	•			*Project Food, Land & People: Resources for Learning*	"Root Root for Life," p. 91: After reading supporting information, students move through stations to observe different types of roots, to learn the ways in which roots help plants, to know the reasons roots are important to people, and to taste the roots.	
			•					*The Growing Classroom*	"Sipping Through a Straw," p. 134: Students observe how colored water moves through a celery stalk.	SCI 2.e
			•					*Project Food, Land & People: Resources for Learning*	"Gifts from the Sun," p. 203: Students read supporting information on photosynthesis and perform skits introducing carbon dioxide, stomata, and other components of photosynthesis.	SCI 2.f, 2.g
				•				*TWIGS*	"Staying Fit with Fiber," p. 105: Students use tubing to simulate an intestine and to compare how foods with varying amounts of fiber move through the model.	

	Standards	Gardening	Nutrition	Cooking	Waste Mgmt.	Ag. Systems	Instructional materials	Activities	Links to other grade 5 standards
Life Sciences	b. Students know how blood circulates through the heart chambers, lungs, and body and how carbon dioxide (CO_2) and oxygen (O_2) are exchanged in the lungs and tissues.	•			•		*Worms Eat Our Garbage*	"'Breathing' Basics," p. 30: Students answer questions by using a diagram to illustrate the exchange of oxygen and carbon dioxide across membranes.	
	e. Students know how sugar, water, and minerals are transported in a vascular plant.	•					*The Growing Classroom*	"Sipping Through a Straw," p. 134: Students observe how colored water moves through a celery stalk.	SCI 2.a
	f. Students know plants use carbon dioxide (CO_2) and energy from sunlight to build molecules of sugar and release oxygen.	•					*The Growing Classroom*	"Plants Need Light Too," p. 139: Students use cork disks to prevent light and air from reaching a section of a leaf, which they then test for starch content.	
		•					*Project Food, Land & People: Resources for Learning*	"Gifts from the Sun," p. 203: Students read supporting information on photosynthesis and perform skits introducing carbon dioxide, stomata, and other components of photosynthesis.	SCI 2.a, 2.g
		•					*Nutrition to Grow On*	"Introduction to Nutrition and Gardening," p. 9, Gardening Activity: To explore photosynthesis, students grow seedlings, varying the amount of light and water for particular plants. Students record their two- to four-week observations of the plants, compare results to those of a control group, and draw conclusions.	

Key: ELA—English–Language Arts; L&S—Listening and Speaking; MATH—Mathematics; M&G—Measurement and Geometry; MR—Mathematical Reasoning; NS—Number Sense; R—Reading; SCI—Science; STATS—Statistics, Data Analysis, and Probability; W—Writing

Table 5.1 Activities that support science standards (Continued)

	Standards		Gardening	Nutrition	Cooking	Waste Mgmt.	Ag. Systems	Instructional materials	Activities	Links to other grade 5 standards
			Content areas							
Life Sciences	2. Plants and animals have structures for respiration, digestion, waste disposal, and transport of materials. As a basis for understanding this concept:	g. Students know plant and animal cells break down sugar to obtain energy, a process resulting in carbon dioxide (CO_2) and water (respiration).	•					*Project Food, Land & People: Resources for Learning*	"Gifts from the Sun," p. 203: Students read supporting information on photosynthesis and perform skits introducing carbon dioxide, stomata, and other components of photosynthesis.	SCI 2.a, 2.f
Earth Sciences	3. Water on Earth moves between the oceans and land through the processes of evaporation and condensation. As a basis for understanding this concept:	a. Students know most of Earth's water is present as salt water in the oceans, which cover most of Earth's surface.					•	*Junior Master Gardener*	"Earth Apple," p. 35: Students divide into sections an apple, which represents the Earth, to illustrate the percentages of land and fresh and salt water.	SCI 3.d MATH NS 1.2
		b. Students know when liquid water evaporates, it turns into water vapor in the air and can reappear as a liquid when cooled or as a solid if cooled below the freezing point of water.	•				•	*Junior Master Gardener*	"Cloud Maker," p. 36: To simulate the formation of rain, students hold a pan of ice over an empty bowl and observe condensation (rain) on the bottom of the pan.	SCI 3.c
		c. Students know water vapor in the air moves from one place to another and can form fog or clouds, which are tiny droplets of water or ice, and can fall to Earth as rain, hail, sleet, or snow.	•				•	*Junior Master Gardener*	"Cloud Maker," p. 36: To simulate the formation of rain, students hold a pan of ice over an empty bowl and observe condensation (rain) on the bottom of the pan.	SCI 3.b

	Standards		Gardening	Nutrition	Cooking	Waste Mgmt.	Ag. Systems	Instructional materials	Activities	Links to other grade 5 standards
Earth Sciences		d. Students know that the amount of fresh water located in rivers, lakes, underground sources, and glaciers is limited and that its availability can be extended by recycling and decreasing the use of water.					•	*Junior Master Gardener*	"Earth Apple," p. 35: Students divide into sections an apple, which represents the Earth, to illustrate the percentages of land and fresh and salt water.	SCI 3.a MATH NS 1.2
							•	*Project Food, Land & People: Resources for Learning*	"Don't Use It All Up!" p. 57: Students drop sponges into a container of water to represent different human demands on available fresh water. They note the drop in water level and then determine ways to conserve water by wringing water from the sponges back into the container and noting the new level of water.	
		e. Students know the origin of the water used by their local communities.	•				•	An activity was not selected from the instructional materials. A general activity is suggested.	Students trace the water in their garden from the hose nozzle to its source. They follow up this investigation with a field trip to the local water utility.	
							•		Students trace the source of water used by local farmers.	
	4. Energy from the Sun heats Earth unevenly, causing air movements that result in changing weather patterns. As a basis for understanding this concept:	b. Students know the influence that the ocean has on the weather and the role that the water cycle plays in weather patterns.					•	An activity was not selected from the instructional materials. A general activity is suggested.	Students study the influence of coastal climate on agricultural production in different parts of the state.	

Key: ELA—English–Language Arts; L&S—Listening and Speaking; MATH—Mathematics; M&G—Measurement and Geometry; MR—Mathematical Reasoning; NS—Number Sense; R—Reading; SCI—Science; STATS—Statistics, Data Analysis, and Probability; W—Writing

Table 5.1 Activities that support science standards (Continued)

Strand	Standards		Gardening	Nutrition	Cooking	Waste Mgmt.	Ag. Systems	Instructional materials	Activities	Links to other grade 5 standards
Investigation and Experimentation	6. Scientific progress is made by asking meaningful questions and conducting careful investigations. As a basis for understanding this concept and addressing the content in the other three strands, students should develop their own questions and perform investigations. Students will:	a. Classify objects (e.g., rocks, plants, leaves) in accordance with appropriate criteria.	•					*Junior Master Gardener*	"Shake, Rattle and Roll," p. 26: Students identify the layers of soil texture, graph the height of layers of particles, and from this graph classify the soil texture.	SCI 1.f MATH A&F 1.1; STATS 1.2
			•					*Junior Master Gardener*	"All in the Family: Insect Flash Cards," p. 80: Students make flash cards to learn the orders of insects by characteristics and Venn diagrams.	
			•					*Junior Master Gardener*	"Ordering Insects," p. 81: Students learn to sort insects by similarities and differences.	
			•					*The Growing Classroom*	"The Nitty-Gritty," p. 73: Students separate soil according to the physical properties of its three main components: sand, silt, and clay.	SCI 1.f
			•			•		*Worms Eat Our Garbage*	"Once a Worm, Always a Worm," p. 13: Students use reference books as their guide to classify worms and insect larva.	
						•		*Worms Eat Our Garbage*	"Classes of Worms," p. 120: Students classify worms according to their habitats and burrowing habits.	
		c. Plan and conduct a simple investigation based on a student-developed question and write instructions others can follow to carry out the procedure.	•					An activity was not selected from the instructional materials. A general activity is suggested.	Students develop a simple investigation to test the relationship between plant growth and environmental factors, such as light and moisture.	SCI 6.e, 6.i

	Standards	Gardening	Nutrition	Cooking	Waste mgmt.	Ag. systems	Instructional materials	Activities	Links to other grade 5 standards
Investigation and Experimentation	d. Identify the dependent and controlled variables in an investigation.	•					*The Growing Classroom*	"Water We Doing?" p. 164: Students observe the relationship between watering and plant growth after discussing the controlled variables.	
	e. Identify a single independent variable in a scientific investigation and explain how this variable can be used to collect information to answer a question about the results of the experiment.	•					An activity was not selected from the instructional materials. A general activity is suggested.	Students develop a simple investigation to test the relationship between plant growth and environmental factors, such as light and moisture.	SCI 6.c, 6.i
	g. Record data by using appropriate graphic representations (including charts, graphs, and labeled diagrams) and make inferences based on those data.	•			•	•	*Kids Cook Farm-Fresh Food*	"Making Compost 'Tea,'" p. 78: Students make compost "tea," a preparation used to improve the soil. They conduct an experiment to determine the effects of adding compost tea to plants. They collect and display the data.	MATH STATS 1.2
	h. Draw conclusions from scientific evidence and indicate whether further information is needed to support a specific conclusion.		•				*Fruits and Vegetables for Health*	"The Chemistry of Fruits and Vegetables," p. 37: Students experiment with fruits and vegetables on how best to store cut produce. They record the results and then discuss and write their conclusions.	SCI 6.i
	i. Write a report of an investigation that includes conducting tests, collecting data or examining evidence, and drawing conclusions		•				*Fruits and Vegetables for Health*	"The Chemistry of Fruits and Vegetables," p. 37: Students experiment with fruits and vegetables on how best to store cut produce. They record the results and then discuss and write their conclusions.	SCI 6.h

Key: ELA—English–Language Arts; L&S—Listening and Speaking; MATH—Mathematics; M&G—Measurement and Geometry; MR—Mathematical Reasoning; NS—Number Sense; R—Reading; SCI—Science; STATS—Statistics, Data Analysis, and Probability; W—Writing

Grade Five / History–Social Science

Table 5.2 Activities that support history–social science standards

NOTE: To view the complete standards, go to <*www.cde.ca.gov/standards/*>.

Standards		Gardening	Nutrition	Cooking	Waste mgmt.	Ag. systems	Instructional materials	Activities	Links to other grade 5 standards
		Content areas							
5.1 Students describe the major pre-Columbian settlements, including the cliff dwellers and pueblo people of the desert Southwest, the American Indians of the Pacific Northwest, the nomadic nations of the Great Plains, and the woodland peoples east of the Mississippi River.	1. Describe how geography and climate influenced the way various nations lived and adjusted to the natural environment, including locations of villages, the distinct structures that they built, and how they obtained food, clothing, tools, and utensils.	•				•	An activity was not selected from the instructional materials. A general activity is suggested.	Students compare crops and agricultural practices in the settlements (e.g., the use of tools) with those used in the school garden.	
		•						Students grow pre-Columbian crops in the school garden.	
	2. Describe their varied customs and folklore traditions.	•					*The Growing Classroom*	"Mother Earth," p. 205: Students read and discuss passages from American Indian writings and speeches in the 1800s.	ELA R 1.1
5.2 Students trace the routes of early explorers and describe the early explorations of the Americas.	3. Trace the routes of the major land explorers of the United States, the distances traveled by explorers, and the Atlantic trade routes that linked Africa, the West Indies, the British colonies, and Europe.					•	An activity was not selected from the instructional materials. A general activity is suggested.	Students map the Atlantic trade routes and label the movement of trade goods. They research the movement of food to and from the U.S. colonies.	
		•				•		Students find the places of origin of crops in the school garden.	
5.3 Students describe the cooperation and conflict that existed among the American Indians and between the Indian nations and the new settlers.	2. Describe the cooperation that existed between the colonists and Indians during the 1600s and 1700s (e.g., in agriculture, the fur trade, military alliances, treaties, cultural interchanges).	•				•	An activity was not selected from the instructional materials. A general activity is suggested.	Students list practices and crops that the settlers and the American Indians shared. They compare their findings to crops in the school garden. Students grow American Indian and settler crops in the school garden.	

Standards		Gardening	Nutrition	Cooking	Waste mgmt.	Ag. systems	Instructional materials	Activities	Links to other grade 5 standards
		Content areas							
5.4 Students understand the political, religious, social, and economic institutions that evolved in the colonial era.	1. Understand the influence of location and physical setting on the founding of the original 13 colonies, and identify on a map the locations of the colonies and of the American Indian nations already inhabiting these areas.					•	An activity was not selected from the instructional materials. A general activity is suggested.	Students research the impact that differences in location and geography had on the production of food in each of the 13 colonies and in American Indian nations.	
	6. Describe the introduction of slavery into America, the responses of slave families to their condition, the ongoing struggle between proponents and opponents of slavery, and the gradual institutionalization of slavery in the South.					•	An activity was not selected from the instructional materials. A general activity is suggested.	Students research crops brought to America by African slaves and crops that thrived due to slave labor.	
		•						Students grow cotton in the school garden.	
5.8 Students trace the colonization, immigration, and settlement patterns of the American people from 1789 to the mid-1800s, with emphasis on the role of economic incentives, effects of the physical and political geography, and transportation systems.	1. Discuss the waves of immigrants from Europe between 1789 and 1850 and their modes of transportation into the Ohio and Mississippi Valleys and through the Cumberland Gap (e.g., overland wagons, canals, flatboats, steamboats).					•	An activity was not selected from the instructional materials. A general activity is suggested.	Students research which crops and farming practices immigrants brought with them and what agricultural opportunities were open to immigrants in the Ohio and Mississippi Valleys.	

Key: ELA—English–Language Arts; L&S—Listening and Speaking; MATH—Mathematics; M&G—Measurement and Geometry; MR—Mathematical Reasoning; NS—Number Sense; R—Reading; SCI—Science; STATS—Statistics, Data Analysis, and Probability; W—Writing

Table 5.2 Activities that support history–social science standards (Continued)

Standards		Gardening	Nutrition	Cooking	Waste Mgmt.	Ag. Systems	Instructional materials	Activities	Links to other grade 5 standards
5.8 Students trace the colonization, immigration, and settlement patterns of the American people from 1789 to the mid-1800s, with emphasis on the role of economic incentives, effects of the physical and political geography, and transportation systems.	4. Discuss the experiences of settlers on the overland trails to the West (e.g., location of the routes; purpose of the journeys; the influence of the terrain, rivers, vegetation, and climate; life in the territories at the end of these trails).					•	An activity was not selected from the instructional materials. A general activity is suggested.	Students find out the settlers' sources of food on their journeys to the West.	
	5. Describe the continued migration of Mexican settlers into Mexican territories of the West and Southwest.					•	An activity was not selected from the instructional materials. A general activity is suggested.	Students research the impact of Mexican immigration on food and food production.	

Grade Five / Mathematics

Table 5.3 Activities that support mathematics standards

NOTE: To view the complete standards, go to <*www.cde.ca.gov/standards/*>.

	Standards		Gardening	Nutrition	Cooking	Waste Mgmt.	Ag. Systems	Instructional materials	Activities	Links to other grade 5 standards
Number Sense	1.0 Students compute with very large and very small numbers, positive integers, decimals, and fractions and understand the relationship between decimals, fractions, and percents. They understand the relative magnitudes of numbers:	1.1 Estimate, round, and manipulate very large (e.g., millions) and very small (e.g., thousandths) numbers.				•		*Worms Eat Our Garbage*	"Weigh in Concepts," p. 133: After reading information on the number of worms in soil, students calculate the answers to questions.	ELA R 2.3
		1.2 Interpret percents as a part of a hundred; find decimal and percent equivalents for common fractions and explain why they represent the same value; compute a given percent of a whole number.				•		*Worms Eat Our Garbage*	"Population of Change," p. 110: Students calculate the percentage change in the population of worms for a number of soil types.	
						•		*Closing the Loop*	"Performing a Class Audit of Waste," p. 321: Students evaluate and record the waste stream over a period of days, then calculate percentages and compare types of waste.	MATH MR 2.6; STATS 1.3
				•				*Nutrition to Grow On*	"Food Labels," p. 79, Nutrition Activities: Students learn to read Nutrition Facts labels and learn how the percentage of daily recommended nutrients in a serving of food is calculated. Using a point card, students compare nutritional values of different foods.	ELA R 2.1
							•	*Junior Master Gardener*	"Earth Apple," p. 35: Students divide into sections an apple, which represents Earth, to illustrate the percentages of land and fresh and salt water.	

Key: ELA—English–Language Arts; L&S—Listening and Speaking; MATH—Mathematics; M&G—Measurement and Geometry; MR—Mathematical Reasoning; NS—Number Sense; R—Reading; SCI—Science; STATS—Statistics, Data Analysis, and Probability; W—Writing

Table 5.3 Activities that support mathematics standards (Continued)

	Standards		Gardening	Nutrition	Cooking	Waste mgmt.	Ag. systems	Instructional materials	Activities	Links to other grade 5 standards
			Content areas							
Number Sense	2.0 Students perform calculations and solve problems involving addition, subtraction, and simple multiplication and division of fractions and decimals:	2.3 Solve simple problems, including ones arising in concrete situations, involving the addition and subtraction of fractions and mixed numbers (like and unlike denominators of 20 or less), and express answers in the simplest form.			•			*Kids Cook Farm-Fresh Food*	Recipes in each section: While following the recipes for preparing food, students determine quantities of ingredients for different numbers of people.	MATH NS 2.5
		2.5 Compute and perform simple multiplication and division of fractions and apply these procedures to solving problems.			•			*Kids Cook Farm-Fresh Food*	Recipes in each section: While following the recipes for preparing food, students determine quantities of ingredients for different numbers of people.	MATH NS 2.3
Algebra and Functions	1.0 Students use variables in simple expressions, compute the value of the expression for specific values of the variable, and plot and interpret the results:	1.1 Use information taken from a graph or equation to answer questions about a problem situation.	•					*Junior Master Gardener*	"Shake, Rattle and Roll," p. 26: Students identify the layers of soil texture and graph the height of layers of particles. From the graph students classify the texture of the soil.	SCI 1.f, 6.a MATH STATS 1.2
						•		*Worms Eat Our Garbage*	"How Many Worms," p. 135: Students interpret graphs and calculate averages.	

Strand	Standards		Gardening	Nutrition	Cooking	Waste mgmt.	Ag. systems	Instructional materials	Activities	Links to other grade 5 standards
			Content areas							
Measurement and Geometry	1.0 Students understand and compute the volumes and areas of simple objects:	1.3 Understand the concept of volume and use the appropriate units in common measuring systems (i.e., cubic centimeter [cm^3], cubic meter [m^3], cubic inch [in^3], cubic yard [yd^3]) to compute the volume of rectangular solids.				•		*Worms Eat Our Garbage*	"Worm Bedding Calculations," p. 71: To find how much bedding is required for their worm bin, students complete certain steps, including measuring a bin and calculating the volume of garbage.	MATH M&G 1.4
						•		*Worms Eat Our Garbage*	"How Big a Bin," p. 70: Students study a chart that indicates how big a bin should be to handle different amounts of garbage and look at pictures indicating different shapes of bins containing the same volume. They then answer questions.	
Statistics, Data Analysis, and Probability	1.0 Students display, analyze, compare, and interpret different data sets, including data sets of different sizes:	1.1 Know the concepts of mean, median, and mode; compute and compare simple examples to show that they may differ.				•		*Worms Eat Our Garbage*	"Wild Worms," p. 134: From data on the weight of worms in different soils, students calculate averages.	
		1.2 Organize and display single-variable data in appropriate graphs and representations (e.g., histogram, circle graphs) and explain which types of graphs are appropriate for various data sets.				•		*Worms Eat Our Garbage*	"Organizing Worms," p. 74: Students analyze a set of data by organizing it into a histogram and bar graph.	
				•				*Project Food, Land & People: Resources for Learning*	"Why I Buy," p. 517: Students read about techniques used in advertising, explore their own buying habits, then write and conduct a survey on peanut butter brands. They graph their findings.	ELA L&S 1.7
					•			*Kids Cook Farm-Fresh Food*	"Frozen, Canned, or Fresh: Which Do You Prefer?" p. 88: Students survey the preferences of students for spinach and determine ways to display their findings.	

Key: ELA—English–Language Arts; L&S—Listening and Speaking; MATH—Mathematics; M&G—Measurement and Geometry; MR—Mathematical Reasoning; NS—Number Sense; R—Reading; SCI—Science; STATS—Statistics, Data Analysis, and Probability; W—Writing

Table 5.3 Activities that support mathematics standards (Continued)

Strand	Standards		Gardening	Nutrition	Cooking	Waste mgmt.	Ag. systems	Instructional materials	Activities	Links to other grade 5 standards
Statistics, Data Analysis, and Probability	1.0 Students display, analyze, compare, and interpret different data sets, including data sets of different sizes:		•			•	•	*Kids Cook Farm-Fresh Food*	"Making Compost 'Tea,'" p. 78: Students make compost "tea," a preparation used to improve the soil. They conduct an experiment to determine the effects of adding compost tea to plants. They collect and display data.	SCI 6.g
				•				*Fruits and Vegetables for Health*	"Nutritional Value of Fresh Produce," p. 27: Students use data provided on vitamin A, vitamin C, and fiber in fruits and vegetables to create bar graphs and analyze the information.	MATH NS 1.2; STATS 1.2
		1.3 Use fractions and percentages to compare data sets of different sizes.				•		*Closing the Loop*	"Performing a Class Audit of Waste, p. 321: Students evaluate and record the waste stream over a period of days, then calculate percentages and compare types of waste.	MATH MR 2.6; NS 1.2
Mathematical Reasoning	2.0 Students use strategies, skills, and concepts in finding solutions:	2.1 Use estimation to verify the reasonableness of calculated results.		•				*Nutrition to Grow On*	"Serving Sizes," p. 59, Nutrition Activities: Students review the Food Guide Pyramid, identify proper serving sizes, compare with familiar objects, calculate the serving size by using measurement tools, and determine what they need to eat for the rest of the day to meet the Food Guide Pyramid recommendations.	

Grade Five / English–Language Arts

Table 5.4 Activities that support English–language arts standards

NOTE: To view the complete standards, go to <*www.cde.ca.gov/standards/*>.

	Standards		Gardening	Nutrition	Cooking	Waste mgmt.	Ag. systems	Instructional materials	Activities	Links to other grade 5 standards
Reading	1.0 Word Analysis, Fluency, and Systematic Vocabulary Development	*Word Recognition* 1.1 Read aloud narrative and expository text fluently and accurately and with appropriate pacing, intonation, and expression.	•					*The Growing Classroom*	"Mother Earth," p. 205: Students read and discuss passages from American Indian writings and speeches in the 1800s.	HSS 5.1.2
							•	*Kids Cook Farm-Fresh Food*	Crop descriptions and farm profiles: Students read about a crop and the small California farm that grows the crop.	ELA R 2.3
	2.0 Reading Comprehension (Focus on Informational Materials)	*Structural Features of Informational Materials* 2.1 Understand how text features (e.g., format, graphics, sequence, diagrams, illustrations, charts, maps) make information accessible and usable.		•				*Nutrition to Grow On*	"Food Labels," p. 79, Nutrition Activities: Students learn to read Nutrition Facts labels and learn how the percentage of daily recommended nutrients in a serving of food is calculated. Using a point card, students compare nutritional values of different foods.	MATH NS 1.2
		Comprehension and Analysis of Grade-Level-Appropriate Text 2.3 Discern main ideas and concepts presented in texts, identifying and assessing evidence that supports those ideas.				•		*Worms Eat Our Garbage*	"Weigh in Concepts," p. 133: After reading information on worms in a soil sample, students answer questions.	MATH NS 1.1
							•	*Worms Eat Our Garbage*	"Rachel Carson," p. 49: Students read a short essay on Rachel Carson and her work and then answer questions	
							•	*Kids Cook Farm-Fresh Food*	Crop descriptions and farm profiles: Students read about a crop and the small California farm that grows the crop. They identify the main ideas and write summaries in their journals.	ELA R 1.1

Key: ELA—English–Language Arts; L&S—Listening and Speaking; MATH—Mathematics; M&G—Measurement and Geometry; MR—Mathematical Reasoning; NS—Number Sense; R—Reading; SCI—Science; STATS—Statistics, Data Analysis, and Probability; W—Writing

Table 5.4 Activities that support English–language arts standards (Continued)

	Standards		Gardening	Nutrition	Cooking	Waste Mgmt.	Ag. Systems	Instructional materials	Activities	Links to other grade 5 standards
Reading	2.0 Reading Comprehension (Focus on Informational Materials)	2.4 Draw inferences, conclusions, or generalizations about text and support them with textual evidence and prior knowledge.	•				•	*Junior Master Gardener*	"Both Sides of the Fence," p. 55: Students read background information on two neighbors who differ in their opinions about the use of chemicals, such as pesticides. They then debate the issue.	ELA L&S 1.5
		Expository Critique 2.5 Distinguish facts, supported inferences, and opinions in text.				•		*Worms Eat Our Garbage*	"Fact or Opinion," p. 111: After reading notes from a fictitious science report, students determine whether statements are fact or opinion.	
							•	*Worms Eat Our Garbage*	"The Worm Gazette," p. 95: Students pick out the humor, quotes, opinion, and facts from a fictitious news article.	
Writing	2.0 Writing Applications (Genres and Their Characteristics)	2.1 Write narratives: a. Establish a plot, point of view, setting, and conflict. b. Show, rather than tell, the events of the story.	•					*Junior Master Gardener*	"Plant Performance," p. 15: In creative writing students develop an understanding of plant needs from the plant's perspective.	
		2.4 Write persuasive letters or compositions: a. State a clear position in support of a proposal. b. Support a position with relevant evidence. c. Follow a simple organizational pattern. d. Address reader concerns.		•		•	•	*Project Food, Land & People: Resources for Learning*	"To Whom It May Concern," p. 351, Option 2: Students read articles on controversial topics of their choice, discern facts from opinion, and write a persuasive letter to a government official. Peers edit their letters, which are presented to the class.	ELA R 2.5

	Standards		Gardening	Nutrition	Cooking	Waste mgmt.	Ag. systems	Instructional materials	Activities	Links to other grade 5 standards
Listening and Speaking	1.0 Listening and Speaking Strategies	*Comprehension* 1.1 Ask questions that seek information not already discussed.					•	*Project Food, Land & People: Resources for Learning*	"Soil's Not Trivial," p. 547: Using facts about the Dust Bowl, students analyze and evaluate information on the history of the Natural Resource Conservation Service and develop a plan for local soil conservation.	ELA L&S 1.5, 2.2; R 2.3
		Organization and Delivery of Oral Communication 1.4 Select a focus, organizational structure, and point of view for an oral presentation.		•				*Project Food, Land & People: Resources for Learning*	"Be Label Able," p. 483: Students compare cereal nutrition labels, determine whether claims on the label are valid, and explain orally their thinking.	
		1.5 Clarify and support spoken ideas with evidence and examples.	•				•	*Junior Master Gardener*	"Both Sides of the Fence," p. 55: Students read background information on two neighbors who differ in their opinions about pesticide use, then debate the issue.	ELA R 2.4
		Analysis and Evaluation of Oral and Media Communications 1.7 Identify, analyze, and critique persuasive techniques (e.g., promises, dares, flattery, glittering generalities); identify logical fallacies used in oral presentations and media messages.	•					*Project Food, Land & People: Resources for Learning*	"Why I Buy," p. 517: Students read an article on techniques used in advertising, explore their own buying habits, then write and conduct a survey on peanut butter brands. They graph their findings.	MATH STATS 1.2
				•				*Nutrition to Grow On*	"Consumerism," p. 127, Nutrition Activities: Students brainstorm various methods in advertising and analyze an advertisement.	

Key: ELA—English–Language Arts; L&S—Listening and Speaking; MATH—Mathematics; M&G—Measurement and Geometry; MR—Mathematical Reasoning; NS—Number Sense; R—Reading; SCI—Science; STATS—Statistics, Data Analysis, and Probability; W—Writing

Grade Six

The clearest links between school gardens and the standards for grade six are in science. Taking a systems perspective, students revisit the life science concepts they learned in previous grades. They study how energy flows and matter cycles through natural systems. In a garden setting students have an opportunity to explore ecological principles and understand the natural resources involved in food production. For the first time students formulate hypotheses.

The history–social science standards require students in grade six to study ancient civilizations and to develop critical thinking by considering where and how civilizations developed. The standards emphasize the study of everyday life. Students who have worked in a school garden know from direct experience the importance of irrigation, maintenance of soil fertility, climate, and plant viability and the usefulness of various tools. They learn what farming practices people in different civilizations used. Because GBE materials currently have very few activities that support the history–social science standards, all but one of the suggested activities are general activities.

In mathematics students master the four arithmetic operations with whole numbers, fractions, decimals, and positive and negative integers. In statistics students learn to determine which measures of central tendency (mean, median, mode) are more useful for a particular data set. They take and analyze samples and work with rates and proportions. Students can generate data sets from garden experiments and from surveys of student attitudes and behaviors, including those involving nutrition habits. They can investigate relationships between variables to show growth rates, plant yields, and profitability in activities that address the algebra and function standards.

English–language arts standards for this grade level require students to read aloud expository and narrative texts as they did in grade five. For the first time standards emphasize analyzing, explaining, and critiquing text rather than merely understanding and describing text. Students write multiple-paragraph expository compositions and write research reports in which they practice English–language arts skills, including computer-based research skills.

"Mustard greens saved our lives in Laos when other crops failed. This is why we must keep growing them and teach them to our children."

—*Mien grandmother*

On a sunny November day, a group of sixth grade students from the Southeast Asian Writing Project could be seen leading tour groups of K–3 students through their families' gardens in search of mustard greens in all six stages of their life cycle. Simultaneously, a group of Mien grandparents and parents assisted each child in planting a handful of mustard green seeds in a cup. These seeds were saved from their family garden plots, which are part of a school-community garden project through which immigrant families from Southeast Asia and Mexico are able to share cultural and nutritional knowledge. In this case, lessons in the garden laid the groundwork for an "ethnic lunch," a stir-fry menu option prepared with the help of Mien parents in the school cafeteria. After the students learned the life cycle of mustard greens, heard a story about what the greens represent in Laos, and planted their own seeds, it was not surprising that the healthful dish of mustard greens with beef and garlic was sold out.

Lorie Hammond, Assistant Professor
California State University, Sacramento
Co-Principal Investigator, Project FIELD
Evergreen School
Washington Unified School District
West Sacramento

Grade Six / Science

Table 6.1 Activities that support science standards

NOTE: To view the complete standards, go to <*www.cde.ca.gov/standards/*>.

	Standards		Content areas: Gardening	Nutrition	Cooking	Waste Mgmt.	Ag. Systems	Instructional materials	Activities	Links to other grade 6 standards
Earth Science: Shaping Earth's Surface	2. Topography is reshaped by the weathering of rock and soil and by the transportation and deposition of sediment. As a basis for understanding this concept:	a. Students know water running downhill is the dominant process in shaping the landscape, including California's landscape.	•				•	*Project Food, Land & People: Resources for Learning*	"Till We or Won't We?" p. 213: Students develop a hypothesis and conduct tests to explore the effects of three soil preparation techniques on water runoff.	SCI 7.a ELA R 2.3
		b. Students know rivers and streams are dynamic systems that erode, transport sediment, change course, and flood their banks in natural and recurring patterns.	•					An activity was not selected from the instructional materials. A general activity is suggested.	Using a hose, students create miniature rivers in the garden and observe the course of water flow and erosion.	
Earth Science: Energy	4. Many phenomena on the Earth's surface are affected by the transfer of energy through radiation and convection currents. As a basis for understanding this concept:	a. Students know the sun is the major source of energy for phenomena on Earth's surface; it powers winds, ocean currents, and the water cycle.	•					*The Growing Classroom*	"Plant Sweat," p. 135: Students conduct an experiment with potted plants to demonstrate transpiration and evaporation of water. Students note the role of the sun in this process.	

Section	Standards		Gardening	Nutrition	Cooking	Waste mgmt.	Ag. systems	Instructional materials	Activities	Links to other grade 6 standards
			Content areas							
Earth Science: Ecology (Life Science)	5. Organisms in ecosystems exchange energy and nutrients among themselves and with the environment. As a basis for understanding this concept:	a. Students know energy entering ecosystems as sunlight is transferred by producers into chemical energy through photosynthesis and then from organism to organism through food webs.	•	•				*Project Food, Land & People: Resources for Learning*	"Gifts from the Sun," p. 203: Students read supporting information on photosynthesis and perform a skit, playing the roles of the sun, roots, chlorophyll, H_2O, CO_2, and stomata.	ELA R 2.3
			•					*Nutrition to Grow On*	"Introduction to Nutrition and Gardening," p. 9, Gardening Activity: Students plant seeds in trays and conduct experiments with light and water to study photosynthesis.	
			•					*The Growing Classroom*	"Sugar Factories," p. 132: Students are introduced to the concept of photosynthesis through the story of Van Helmont's experiment conducted 350 years ago.	
		b. Students know matter is transferred over time from one organism to others in the food web and between organisms and the physical environment.	•			•		*The Growing Classroom*	"Let's Make a Compost Cake," p. 199: Students build a compost pile and observe the transformation of matter over time.	
					•			*Kids Cook Farm-Fresh Food*	"Comparative Tasting Format," p. xviii: Students try several varieties of a fruit or vegetable and learn that matter is being transferred from one organism to another during the act of eating.	SCI 5.a
			•			•		*Nutrition to Grow On*	"Nutrients We Need," p. 27, Gardening Activity: Students make worm composting systems in bottles and observe the transformation of food scraps into soil amendments for new plant growth.	

Key: A&F—Algebra and Functions; ELA—English–Language Arts; HSS—History–Social Science; MATH—Mathematics; MR—Mathematical Reasoning; NS—Number Sense; R—Reading; SCI—Science; STATS—Statistics, Data Analysis, and Probability; W—Writing

Table 6.1 Activities that support science standards (Continued)

	Standards		Gardening	Nutrition	Cooking	Waste Mgmt.	Ag. Systems	Instructional materials	Activities	Links to other grade 6 standards
Earth Science: Ecology (Life Science)	5. Organisms in ecosystems exchange energy and nutrients among themselves and with the environment. As a basis for understanding this concept:	b. Students know matter is transferred over time from one organism to others in the food web and between organisms and the physical environment.	•			•		*Worms Eat Our Garbage*	"Worm Water Tea," p. 126: Students conduct an experiment to study the effects that worm castings and water have on plant growth over a four-week period.	SCI 5.e
			•			•		*Worms Eat Our Garbage*	"Food Web of the Compost Pile," p. 89: Students study a diagram defining three levels of consumers in a compost pile, then answer questions on that information.	SCI 5.c
			•			•		*Closing the Loop*	"The Nutrient Cycle and Other Cycles," p. 451: Students collect and bury leaves and develop a hypothesis about what will happen to the leaves. They observe the changes that occur over time.	SCI 7.a
		c. Students know populations of organisms can be categorized by the functions they serve in an ecosystem.	•					*Project Food, Land & People: Resources for Learning*	"Investigating Insects," p. 181: Students learn the structure and function of insects. They conduct observations of insects at different times throughout the year and record their observations. Students play a game to learn about the helpful behaviors of five beneficial insects.	
			•			•	•	*Project Food, Land & People: Resources for Learning*	"From Apple Cores to Healthy Soil," p. 111: After identifying and discussing decomposers and demonstrating the nutrient cycle, students build two small-scale compost systems. They add water to only one and observe the differences in decomposition rates.	SCI 5.e, 7.e

	Standards		Gardening	Nutrition	Cooking	Waste mgmt.	Ag. systems	Instructional materials	Activities	Links to other grade 6 standards
Earth Science: Ecology (Life Science)			•				•	*What's Bugging You?*	"Quit Pestering Us!" p. 11: Students are divided into six groups. Each group reads an information page about a garden pest and pest-management solutions. Each group presents its findings to the class.	
			•			•	•	*Worms Eat Our Garbage*	"Food Web of the Compost Pile," p. 89: After studying a diagram defining three levels of consumers in a compost pile, students answer questions on that information.	SCI 5.b
		e. Students know the number and types of organisms an ecosystem can support depends on the resources available and on abiotic factors, such as quantities of light and water, a range of temperatures, and soil composition.					•	*Kids Cook Farm-Fresh Food*	"Crop Rotation," p. 144: Students learn how farms improve soil composition by rotating crops to maintain plant production.	SCI 6.b
							•	*Project Food, Land & People: Resources for Learning*	"What Will the Land Support?" p. 337: Students play a board game that simulates the capacity of land to support the population. They observe the effects of increases in population.	SCI 6.b MATH STATS 3.2
Earth Science: Resources	6. Sources of energy and materials differ in amounts, distribution, usefulness, and the time required for their formation. As a basis for understanding this concept:	a. Students know the utility of energy sources is determined by factors that are involved in converting these sources to useful forms and the consequences of the conversion process.					•	An activity was not selected from the instructional materials. A general activity is suggested.	Students diagram the paths an apple takes to the classroom from the school garden, a California farm, or China, labeling the sources of energy used. Students discuss the sources of energy used in the transportation and some of the consequences of the conversion process.	

Key: A&F—Algebra and Functions; ELA—English–Language Arts; HSS—History–Social Science; MATH—Mathematics; MR—Mathematical Reasoning; NS—Number Sense; R—Reading; SCI—Science; STATS—Statistics, Data Analysis, and Probability; W—Writing

Table 6.1 Activities that support science standards (Continued)

Strand	Standards		Gardening	Nutrition	Cooking	Waste Mgmt.	Ag. Systems	Instructional materials	Activities	Links to other grade 6 standards
Earth Science: Resources	6. Sources of energy and materials differ in amounts, distribution, usefulness, and the time required for their formation. As a basis for understanding this concept:	b. Students know different natural energy and material resources, including air, soil, rocks, minerals, petroleum, fresh water, wildlife, and forests, and know how to classify them as renewable or nonrenewable.				•	•	*Closing the Loop*	"Away to the Landfill," p. 259: Students discuss different kinds of renewable and nonrenewable resources and build a landfill in a bottle.	
			•				•	*Project Food, Land & People: Resources for Learning*	"Don't Use It All Up!" p. 57: Students discuss the availability of fresh water on Earth. They do an activity that shows the limited supply of fresh water available for human use, including water for agriculture. Students graph data showing how Earth's total water supply is stored.	SCI 7.c ELA R 2.3
Investigation and Experimentation	7. Scientific progress is made by asking meaningful questions and conducting careful investigations. As a basis for understanding this concept and addressing the content in the other three strands, students should develop their own questions and perform investigations. Students will:	a. Develop a hypothesis.	•			•		*Closing the Loop*	"The Nutrient Cycle and Other Cycles," p. 451: Students collect and bury leaves and develop a hypothesis about what will happen to the leaves. They observe the changes that occur over time.	SCI 5.b
				•			•	*Project Food, Land & People: Resources for Learning*	"Why I Buy," p. 517: Students discuss techniques used in advertising and explore reasons for their own buying habits. They develop a hypothesis on factors determining consumer choice of peanut butter, create a survey to test the hypothesis, collect data, and graph and analyze their findings.	SCI 7.c, 7.d ELA R 2.3
			•				•	*Project Food, Land & People: Resources for Learning*	"Till We or Won't We?" p. 213: Students develop a hypothesis and conduct tests to explore the effects of soil preparation techniques on water runoff.	SCI 2.a ELA R 2.3

	Standards	Gardening	Nutrition	Cooking	Waste Mgmt.	Ag. Systems	Instructional materials	Activities	Links to other grade 6 standards
Investigation and Experimentation	b. Select and use appropriate tools and technology (including calculators, computers, balances, spring scales, microscopes, and binoculars) to perform tests, collect data, and display data.				•		*Closing the Loop*	"Performing a Class Audit of Waste," p. 321: Students use scales to measure classroom waste over one week, calculate the percentage of each type of waste, graph their findings, and develop a plan to reduce waste.	
						•	*Project Food, Land & People: Resources for Learning*	"Go, Go H_2O!" p. 561: Students discuss ancient water systems and modern irrigation methods. They construct model irrigation systems. Students develop a plan to evaluate the efficiency of their system, conduct the evaluation, and share their findings.	SCI 5.e, 6.b, 7.d HSS 6.2.2
	c. Construct appropriate graphs from data and develop qualitative statements about the relationships between variables.					•	*Project Food, Land & People: Resources for Learning*	"Global Grocery Bags," p. 527: Students read about the cost of groceries in different countries. They compare statistics on different countries' food consumption and food costs. Students graph their findings and look for patterns in the relationship between income level and the percentage of income spent on food.	MATH MR 2.5 ELA R 2.3
		•				•	*Project Food, Land & People: Resources for Learning*	"Don't Use It All Up!" p. 57: Students discuss the availability of fresh water on Earth. They do an activity that shows the limited supply of fresh water available for human use, including water for agriculture. Students graph data showing how Earth's total water supply is stored.	SCI 6.b ELA R 2.3

Key: A&F—Algebra and Functions; ELA—English–Language Arts; HSS—History–Social Science; MATH—Mathematics; MR—Mathematical Reasoning; NS—Number Sense; R—Reading; SCI—Science; STATS—Statistics, Data Analysis, and Probability; W—Writing

Table 6.1 Activities that support science standards (Continued)

Strand	Standards		Gardening	Nutrition	Cooking	Waste Mgmt.	Ag. Systems	Instructional materials	Activities	Links to other grade 6 standards
Investigation and Experimentation	7. Scientific progress is made by asking meaningful questions and conducting careful investigations. As a basis for understanding this concept and addressing the content in the other three strands, students should develop their own questions and perform investigations. Students will:	e. Recognize whether evidence is consistent with a proposed explanation.		•			•	*Project Food, Land & People: Resources for Learning*	"Be Label Able," p. 483: Students read cereal nutrition labels to compare the number of grams of fat, fiber, sugar, and sodium contained in the products. They graph their findings and rank various foods according to nutritional value. They determine whether nutritional health claims on the box are valid and explain their thinking in oral presentations.	MATH MR 2.4, 2.5; STATS 2.5 ELA R 2.8
		f. Read a topographic map and a geologic map for evidence provided on the maps and construct and interpret a simple scale map.	•					An activity was not selected from the instructional materials. A general activity is suggested.	Students read a topographic map and a geologic map of their region. They measure the perimeter of the school garden and construct a map to scale. They add contour lines where appropriate.	
		h. Identify changes in natural phenomena over time without manipulating the phenomena (e.g., a tree limb, a grove of trees, a stream, a hill slope).	•					*The Growing Classroom*	"Adopt-a-Tree," p.177: Students observe and record seasonal changes in the life of a tree.	

Grade Six / History–Social Science

Table 6.2 Activities that support history–social science standards

NOTE: To view the complete standards, go to <*www.cde.ca.gov/standards/*>.

Standards		Content areas: Gardening	Nutrition	Cooking	Waste Mgmt.	Ag. Systems	Instructional materials	Activities	Links to other grade 6 standards
6.1 Students describe what is known through archaeological studies of the early physical and cultural development of humankind from the Paleolithic era to the agricultural revolution.	1. Describe the hunter-gatherer societies, including the development of tools and the use of fire.					•	An activity was not selected from the instructional materials. A general activity is suggested.	Students research hunter-gatherers' foods and methods for obtaining food, including the use of tools.	
6.2 Students analyze the geographic, political, economic, religious, and social structures of the early civilizations of Mesopotamia, Egypt, and Kush.	1. Locate and describe the major river systems and discuss the physical settings that supported permanent settlement and early civilizations.					•	An activity was not selected from the instructional materials. A general activity is suggested.	Students research the connection between river systems and the development of agriculture in Egypt, Mesopotamia, and Kush.	SCI 2.b
		•				•		Students describe the physical setting of the school garden, looking at water sources, soil type, and topography. They do the same for the civilizations of Egypt, Mesopotamia, and Kush, then compare findings.	
	2. Trace the development of agricultural techniques that permitted the production of economic surplus and the emergence of cities as centers of culture and power.					•	*Project Food, Land & People: Resources for Learning*	"Go, Go H_2O!" p. 561: Students discuss ancient water systems and modern irrigation methods. They construct model irrigation systems. Students develop a plan to evaluate the efficiency of their system, conduct the evaluation, and share their findings.	SCI 5.e, 6.b, 7.b, 7.d

Key: A&F—Algebra and Functions; ELA—English–Language Arts; HSS—History–Social Science; MATH—Mathematics; MR—Mathematical Reasoning; NS—Number Sense; R—Reading; SCI—Science; STATS—Statistics, Data Analysis, and Probability; W—Writing

Table 6.2 Activities that support history–social science standards (Continued)

Standards		Content areas: Gardening	Nutrition	Cooking	Waste Mgmt.	Ag. Systems	Instructional materials	Activities	Links to other grade 6 standards
6.2 Students analyze the geographic, political, economic, religious, and social structures of the early civilizations of Mesopotamia, Egypt, and Kush.	6. Describe the role of Egyptian trade in the eastern Mediterranean and Nile valley.	•				•	An activity was not selected from the instructional materials. A general activity is suggested.	Students grow papyrus and learn about its importance in the development of paper. They research the role of papyrus in Egyptian trade.	HSS 6.2.8
	8. Identify the location of the Kush civilization and describe its political, commercial, and cultural relations with Egypt.	•				•	An activity was not selected from the instructional materials. A general activity is suggested.	Students research food traded between Kush and Egypt. They determine whether any of these foods grow in the school garden or the region.	HSS 6.2.7
6.3 Students analyze the geographic, political, economic, religious, and social structures of the Ancient Hebrews.	4. Discuss the locations of the settlements and movements of Hebrew peoples, including the Exodus and their movement to and from Egypt, and outline the significance of the Exodus to the Jewish and other people.	•				•	An activity was not selected from the instructional materials. A general activity is suggested.	Students research food sources and methods of obtaining food in Hebrew settlements. They compare agricultural techniques used by the Hebrews to those used in the school garden.	
6.4 Students analyze the geographic, political, economic, religious, and social structures of the early civilizations of Ancient Greece.	1. Discuss the connections between geography and the development of city-states in the region of the Aegean Sea, including patterns of trade and commerce among Greek city-states and within the wider Mediterranean region.					•	An activity was not selected from the instructional materials. A general activity is suggested.	Students study the impact of geography on agriculture in Ancient Greece and, in turn, on the need to develop trade. Students research what crops Ancient Greeks grew and what crops they obtained through trade.	
						•		Students learn which foods grown in Ancient Greece are now grown in California.	

Standards		Content areas					Instructional materials	Activities	Links to other grade 6 standards
		Gardening	Nutrition	Cooking	Waste mgmt.	Ag. systems			
	4. Explain the significance of Greek mythology to the every-day life of people in the region and how Greek literature continues to permeate our literature and language today, drawing from Greek mythology and epics, such as Homer's *Iliad* and *Odyssey,* and from *Aesop's Fables.*					•	An activity was not selected from the instructional materials. A general activity is suggested.	In their study of Greek mythology, students learn how the Greeks explained everyday occurrences related to agriculture, such as the changing of seasons through the myth of Demeter and Persephone.	
6.5 Students analyze the geographic, political, economic, religious, and social structures of the early civilizations of India.	1. Locate and describe the major river system and discuss the physical setting that supported the rise of this civilization.					•	An activity was not selected from the instructional materials. A general activity is suggested.	Students map the major river systems of ancient India and research the connection between river systems and the development of agriculture and, in turn, the rise of civilization in ancient India.	
		•				•		Students compare how soil fertility was maintained in the Indus Valley to how soil fertility is maintained in the school garden.	
						•		Students learn which foods from ancient India are now grown in California.	

Key: A&F—Algebra and Functions; ELA—English–Language Arts; HSS—History–Social Science; MATH—Mathematics; MR—Mathematical Reasoning; NS—Number Sense; R—Reading; SCI—Science; STATS—Statistics, Data Analysis, and Probability; W—Writing

Table 6.2 Activities that support history–social science standards (Continued)

Standards		Gardening	Nutrition	Cooking	Waste Mgmt.	Ag. Systems	Instructional materials	Activities	Links to other grade 6 standards
6.6 Students analyze the geographic, political, economic, religious, and social structures of the early civilizations of China.	1. Locate and describe the origins of Chinese civilization in the Huang-He Valley during the Shang Dynasty.					•	An activity was not selected from the instructional materials. A general activity is suggested.	Students map the Huang-He River of ancient China. They research the connection between the river system and the development of agriculture and, in turn, the rise of civilization in ancient China.	
		•				•		Students compare how soil fertility was maintained in the Huang-He Valley to how soil fertility is maintained in the school garden.	
						•		Students learn which foods from the Huang-He Valley are now grown in California.	
6.7 Students analyze the geographic, political, economic, religious, and social structures during the development of Rome.	1. Identify the location and describe the rise of the Roman Republic, including the importance of such mythical and historical figures as Aeneas, Romulus and Remus, Cincinnatus, Julius Caesar, and Cicero.					•	An activity was not selected from the instructional materials. A general activity is suggested.	Students research the place of agriculture in the Roman economy. They study the challenges around growing enough food to support the cities and the territories and the subsequent need to develop trade. Students learn what crops Romans grew and what crops they obtained through trade.	
						•		Students examine how the heavy taxation on grains impacted the development of the economy.	
						•		Students learn which foods from the Roman Empire are now grown in California.	

Grade Six / Mathematics

Table 6.3 Activities that support mathematics standards

NOTE: To view the complete standards, go to <*www.cde.ca.gov/standards/*>.

	Standards		Gardening	Nutrition	Cooking	Waste mgmt.	Ag. systems	Instructional materials	Activities	Links to other grade 6 standards
Number Sense	2.0 Students calculate and solve problems involving addition, subtraction, multiplication, and division:	2.3 Solve addition, subtraction, multiplication, and division problems, including those arising in concrete situations that use positive and negative integers and combinations of these operations.	•				•	*Kids Cook Farm-Fresh Food*	"A School Produce Stand," p. 66: Students discuss marketing options for farmers, including farmers markets and produce stands. They develop a plan to sell produce from the garden, determine prices, and make the calculations involved in transactions.	MATH MR 2.7
							•	*Kids Cook Farm-Fresh Food*	"Calculating Farm Profit or Loss," p. 100: Students work with a balance sheet for broccoli production. They calculate profit/loss for varying quantities and varying prices. They determine the cost per box to break even.	MATH A&F 2.2; MR 2.7
Algebra and Functions	1.0 Students write verbal expressions and sentences as algebraic expressions and equations; they evaluate algebraic expressions, solve simple linear equations, and graph and interpret their results:	1.1 Write and solve one-step linear equations in one variable.				•		*Worms Eat Our Garbage*	"Garbage Math," p. 69: Students solve problems using equations to determine the average amount of food waste per day. They are given a problem and write their own equation for a solution.	

Key: A&F—Algebra and Functions; ELA—English–Language Arts; HSS—History–Social Science; MATH—Mathematics; MR—Mathematical Reasoning; NS—Number Sense; R—Reading; SCI—Science; STATS—Statistics, Data Analysis, and Probability; W—Writing

Table 6.3 Activities that support mathematics standards (Continued)

Strand	Standards		Gardening	Nutrition	Cooking	Waste Mgmt.	Ag. Systems	Instructional materials	Activities	Links to other grade 6 standards
Algebra and Functions	2.0 Students analyze and use tables, graphs, and rules to solve problems involving rates and proportions:	2.1 Convert one unit of measurement to another (e.g., from feet to miles, from centimeters to inches).				•		*Worms Eat Our Garbage*	"Worm Weigh In," p. 132: Students read an article on replenishing soil with worm castings. They answer questions and perform calculations.	
		2.2 Demonstrate an understanding that *rate* is a measure of one quantity per unit value of another quantity.					•	*Kids Cook Farm-Fresh Food*	"Calculating Farm Profit or Loss," p. 100: Students work with a balance sheet for broccoli production. They calculate profit/loss for varying quantities and varying prices. They determine the cost per box to break even.	MATH MR 2.7; NS 2.3
			•			•		*Worms Eat Our Garbage*	"How Much Garbage?" p. 65: Students collect classroom food waste over three weeks. They determine the average amount of garbage produced in one week and, using the rate of worm consumption of organic waste, determine the quantity of worms needed for their project.	MATH A&F 2.1
						•		*Worms Eat Our Garbage*	"Worm/Garbage Ratio," p. 67: Students solve problems involving the ratio of the weight of worms to the amount of garbage processed.	MATH A&F 2.1
		2.3 Solve problems involving rates, average speed, distance, and time.	•			•	•	*Worms Eat Our Garbage*	"Worm City Story," p. 152: Students solve problems using rates to determine the amount of money that a city could save in one year by using worm composting.	MATH A&F 2.2; MR 2.7

	Standards		Content areas: Gardening	Nutrition	Cooking	Waste mgmt.	Ag. systems	Instructional materials	Activities	Links to other grade 6 standards
Statistics, Data Analysis, and Probability	1.0 Students compute and analyze statistical measurements for data sets:	1.1 Compute the range, mean, median, and mode of data sets.					•	*Project Food, Land & People: Resources for Learning*	"What Piece of the Pie?" p. 499: Students discuss the many factors that determine the cost of food. They make predictions on food production costs; graph their predictions; determine mean, median, and mode of the data; and compare their predictions to the U.S. Department of Agriculture's analysis.	MATH MR. 2.4, 2.5 ELA R 2.3
	2.0 Students use data samples of a population and describe the characteristics and limitations of the samples:	2.5 Identify claims based on statistical data and, in simple cases, evaluate the validity of the claims.		•				*Project Food, Land & People: Resources for Learning*	"Be Label Able," p. 483: Students read cereal nutrition labels to compare the number of grams of fat, fiber, sugar, and sodium in the products. They graph their findings and rank various foods according to nutritional value. They determine whether nutritional health claims on the box are valid and explain their thinking in oral presentations.	SCI 7.e MATH MR 2.4, 2.5 ELA R 2.8
Mathematical Reasoning	2.0 Students use strategies, skills, and concepts in finding solutions:	2.5 Express the solution clearly and logically by using the appropriate mathematical notation and terms and clear language; support solutions with evidence in both verbal and symbolic work.					•	*Project Food, Land & People: Resources for Learning*	"Global Grocery Bags," p. 527: Students compare statistics on different countries' food consumption and food costs. Students graph their findings and look for patterns in the relationship between income level and the percentage of income spent on food.	SCI 7.c ELA R 2.3
		2.7 Make precise calculations and check the validity of the results from the context of the problem.					•	*Kids Cook Farm-Fresh Food*	"Calculating Farm Profit or Loss," p. 100: Students work with a balance sheet for broccoli production. They calculate profit/loss for varying quantities and varying prices. They determine the cost per box to break even.	MATH A&F 2.2; NS 2.3

Key: A&F—Algebra and Functions; ELA—English–Language Arts; HSS—History–Social Science; MATH—Mathematics; MR—Mathematical Reasoning; NS—Number Sense; R—Reading; SCI—Science; STATS—Statistics, Data Analysis, and Probability; W—Writing

Grade Six / English–Language Arts

Table 6.4 Activities that support English–language arts standards

NOTE: To view the complete standards, go to <*www.cde.ca.gov/standards/*>.

	Standards		Gardening	Nutrition	Cooking	Waste Mgmt.	Ag. Systems	Instructional materials	Activities	Links to other grade 6 standards
Reading	1.0 Word Analysis, Fluency, and Systematic Vocabulary Development	*Word Recognition* 1.1 Read aloud narrative and expository text fluently and accurately and with appropriate pacing, intonation, and expression.					•	*Kids Cook Farm-Fresh Food*	Farm profiles: Students read a farm profile from one or more of the chapters. Each profile tells the story of a farm that grows the crop discussed in the chapter.	ELA R 2.4
	2.0 Reading Comprehension (Focus on Informational Materials)	*Structural Features of Informational Materials* 2.1 Identify the structural features of popular media (e.g., newspapers, magazines, online information) and use the features to obtain information.		•				*Nutrition to Grow On*	"Consumerism," p. 127, Nutrition Activities: Students discuss advertising techniques used by the food industry, analyze a magazine food advertisement, and design an advertisement for a fresh fruit or vegetable.	ELA R 2.8
		Comprehension and Analysis of Grade-Level-Appropriate Text 2.3 Connect and clarify main ideas by identifying their relationships to other sources and related topics.					•	*Project Food, Land & People: Resources for Learning*	"Till We or Won't We?" p. 213: Students read supporting information on soil. They develop a hypothesis and conduct tests to explore the effects of soil preparation techniques on water runoff.	SCI 2.a, 7.a
							•	*Project Food, Land & People: Resources for Learning*	"What Piece of the Pie?" p. 499: Students read supporting information on factors that determine the cost of food. They make predictions on food production costs; graph their predictions; determine mean, median, and mode of the data; and compare their predictions to the U.S. Department of Agriculture's analysis.	MATH MR 2.4, 2.5; STAT 1.1

	Standards	Gardening	Nutrition	Cooking	Waste mgmt.	Ag. systems	Instructional materials	Activities	Links to other grade 6 standards
Reading						•	*Project Food, Land & People: Resources for Learning*	"Global Grocery Bags," p. 527: Students read about the cost of groceries in different countries. They compare statistics on different countries' food consumption and costs. Students graph their findings and look for patterns in the relationship between income level and the percentage of income spent on food.	SCI 7.c MATH MR 2.5
		•			•		*Worms Eat Our Garbage*	"Worm Weigh-In," p. 132: Students read an article on replenishing soil with worm castings. They answer questions on the information contained in the article.	
						•	*Project Food, Land & People: Resources for Learning*	"Why I Buy," p. 517: Students read supporting information on techniques used in advertising and explore reasons for their own buying habits. They develop a hypothesis on factors determining consumer choice of peanut butter, create a survey to test the hypothesis, collect data, and graph and analyze their findings.	SCI 7.a, 7.c, 7.d
	Comprehension and Analysis of Grade-Level-Appropriate Text 2.4 Clarify an understanding of texts by creating outlines, logical notes, summaries, or reports.					•	*Kids Cook Farm-Fresh Food*	Farm profiles: Students read a farm profile from one or more of the chapters. Each profile tells the story of a farm that grows the crop discussed in the chapter. Students identify the main ideas and write summaries in their journals.	ELA R 1.1
	Expository Critique 2.8 Note instances of unsupported inferences, fallacious reasoning, persuasion, and propaganda in text.		•				*Nutrition to Grow On*	"Consumerism," p. 127, Nutrition Activities: Students discuss advertising techniques used by the food industry, analyze a magazine food advertisement, and design an advertisement for a fresh fruit or vegetable.	ELA R 2.1

Key: A&F—Algebra and Functions; ELA—English–Language Arts; HSS—History–Social Science; MATH—Mathematics; MR—Mathematical Reasoning; NS—Number Sense; R—Reading; SCI—Science; STATS—Statistics, Data Analysis, and Probability; W—Writing

Table 6.4 Activities that support English–language arts standards (Continued)

	Standards		Gardening	Nutrition	Cooking	Waste mgmt.	Ag. systems	Instructional materials	Activities	Links to other grade 6 standards
Writing	1.0 Writing Strategies	*Evaluation and Revision* 1.6 Revise writing to improve the organization and consistency of ideas within and between paragraphs.					•	*Project Food, Land & People: Resources for Learning*	"To Whom It May Concern," p. 351, Option 2: Students research a controversial topic of their choosing. They discern facts from opinions and write a persuasive letter to a government official. The letter goes through a peer editing and revision process. Students present their letters to the class.	ELA R 2.3, 2.4, 2.6; W 2.5
Writing	2.0 Writing Applications (Genres and Their Characteristics)	2.3 Write research reports: a. Pose relevant questions with a scope narrow enough to be thoroughly covered. b. Support the main idea or ideas with facts, details, examples, and explanations from multiple authoritative sources (e.g., speakers, periodicals, online information searches). c. Include a bibliography.				•	•	*Closing the Loop*	"Defining Natural Resources," p. 247: Students use a structured format with prompts to write a five-paragraph report on human use of a natural resource.	

	Standards		Content areas: Gardening	Nutrition	Cooking	Waste mgmt.	Ag. systems	Instructional materials	Activities	Links to other grade 6 standards
Writing		2.5 Write persuasive compositions: a. State a clear position on a proposition or proposal. b. Support the position with organized and relevant evidence. c. Anticipate and address reader concerns and counterarguments.					•	*Project Food, Land & People: Resources for Learning*	"To Whom It May Concern," p. 351, Option 2: Students research a controversial topic of their choosing. They discern facts from opinions and write a persuasive letter to a government official. The letter goes through a peer editing and revision process. Students present their letters to the class.	ELA R 2.3, 2.4, 2.6; W 1.6
Listening and Speaking	1.0 Listening and Speaking Strategies	*Analysis and Evaluation of Oral and Media Communications* 1.9 Identify persuasive and propaganda techniques used in television and identify false and misleading information.					•	*Project Food, Land & People: Resources for Learning*	"Why I Buy," p. 517: Students discuss techniques used in advertising and explore reasons for their own buying habits. They develop a hypothesis on factors determining consumer choice of peanut butter, create a survey to test the hypothesis, collect data, and graph and analyze their findings.	SCI 7.a, 7.c, 7.d ELA R 2.3

Key: A&F—Algebra and Functions; ELA—English–Language Arts; HSS—History–Social Science; MATH—Mathematics; MR—Mathematical Reasoning; NS—Number Sense; R—Reading; SCI—Science; STATS—Statistics, Data Analysis, and Probability; W—Writing

SELECTED CHILDREN'S BOOKS

Alphabet Soup, by Kate Banks (K–3)
Ancient Agriculture: From Foraging to Farming, by Mary Woods and Michael Woods (5–8)
Apples and Pumpkins, by Anne Rockwell (K–3)
The Berry Book, by Gail Gibbons (K–3)
Black Potatoes: The Story of the Great Irish Famine, 1845–1850, by Susan Campbell Bartoletti (5–8)
Blueberries for Sal, by Robert McCloskey (K–3)
Blue Potatoes, Orange Tomatoes, by Rosalind Creasy (3–6)
Bread, Bread, Bread, by Ann Morris (K–3)
Bug Watching with Charles Henry Turner, by Michael Ross (3–6)
Buried Treasure: Roots and Tubers, by Meredith Hughes and Tom Hughes (5–8)
The Carrot Seed, by Ruth Krauss (K–3)
City Green, by DyAnne DiSalvo-Ryan (K–3)
Cook-a-Doodle-Doo! by Janet Stevens and Susan Stevens Crummel (K–3)
Cool as a Cucumber, Hot as a Pepper: Fruit Vegetables, by Meredith Hughes (5–8)
Corn Is Maize: The Gift of the Indians, by Aliki (K–3)
The Dandelion Seed, by Joseph Anthony (K–3)
Down to Earth, by Michael Rosen (3–6)
Each Orange Had 8 Slices: A Counting Book, by Paul Giganti, Jr. (K–3)
Eating Fractions, by Bruce McMillan (K–3)
Everyone Bakes Bread, by Norah Dooley (K–3)
Everybody Cooks Rice, by Norah Dooley (K–3)
Farmer Enno and His Cow, by Jens Rassmus (K–3)
Food and Farming, Ancient Egypt Series, by Jane Shuter (K–3)
Farmers Market, by Paul Brett Johnson (K–3)
Flavor Foods: Spices and Herbs, by Meredith Hughes (5–8)
The Garden of Happiness, by Erika Tamar (K–3)
The Gardener, by Sarah Stewart (K–4)
A Gardener's Alphabet, by Mary Azarian (K–3)
George Washington Carver, by Lois Nicholson (3–6)
George Washington Carver: The Peanut Scientist, by Patricia McKissack and Fredrick McKissack (K–3)
The Giant Carrot, by Jan Peck (K–3)
Glorious Grasses: The Grains, by Meredith Hughes (5–8)
Good Bugs for Your Garden, by Allison Starcher (5–8)
Good Enough to Eat, by Lizzy Rockwell (K–3)
Grandpa's Garden, by Shea Darian (K–3)
Green Power: Leaf and Flower Vegetables, by Meredith Hughes (5–8)
The Green Truck Garden Giveaway: A Neighborhood Story and Almanac, by Jacqueline Briggs Martin (K–3)
Gregory, the Terrible Eater, by Mitchell Sharmat (K–3)
Growing Vegetable Soup, by Lois Ehlert (K–3)
Hard to Crack: Nut Trees, by Meredith Hughes (5–8)
A Handful of Seeds, by Monica Hughes (K–3)
Haystack, by Bonnie Geisert and Arthur Geisert (K–3)
Herman and Marguerite: An Earth Story, by Jay O'Callahan (K–3)
How a Seed Grows, by Helene Jordan (K–3)
How Are You Peeling? Foods with Moods, by Saxton Freymann and Joost Elffers (K–3)
How My Parents Learned to Eat, by Ina Friedman (K–3)
In the Garden, by David Schwartz (K–3)
It Could Still Be a Worm, by Allan Fowler (K–4)
Johnny Appleseed, by Eva Moore (3–6)
Johnny Appleseed: My Story, by David Lee Harrison (K–3)
Let's Eat, by Ana Zamorano (K–3)
Linnea's Windowsill Garden, by Christina Bjork (3–6)
Little Farm by the Sea, by Kay Chorao (K–3)
The Little Red Hen, by Lucinda McQueen (K–3)
Miss Rumphius, by Barbara Cooney (K–3)
Oliver's Fruit Salad, by Vivian French (K–3)
Oliver's Vegetables, by Vivian French (K–3)
Once upon MacDonald's Farm, by Stephen Gammell (K–3)
One Grain of Rice: A Mathematical Folktale, by Demi (K–3)
Out of the Dust, by Karen Hesse (3–6)
Pumpkin Circle: The Story of a Garden, by George Levenson (K–3)
Pumpkins: A Story for a Field, by Mary Lyn Ray (K–3)
The Reason for a Flower, by Ruth Heller (K–3)
Round the Garden, by Omri Glaser (K–3)
Saturday Sancocho, by Leyla Torres (K–3)
The Seasons of Arnold's Apple Tree, by Gail Gibbons (K–3)
Seedfolks, by Paul Fleischman (5–8)
Slugs, Bugs and Salamanders: Discovering Animals in Your Garden, by Sally Stenhouse Kneidel (3–6)
Spill the Beans and Pass the Peanuts: Legumes, by Meredith S. Hughes (5–8)
Stinky and Stringy: Stem and Bulb Vegetables, by Meredith Hughes (5–8)
Stone Soup, by Marcia Brown (K–3)
Story of Johnny Appleseed, by Aliki (K–3)
Tall and Tasty: Fruit Trees, by Meredith S. Hughes (5–8)
There's a Hair in My Dirt! A Worm's Story, by Gary Larson (5–8)
Tiny Green Thumbs, by C. Z. Guest (K–3)
Tomatoes, Potatoes, Corn, and Beans: How the Foods of the Americas Changed Eating Around the World, by Sylvia A. Johnson (5–8)
Tops and Bottoms, by Janet Stevens (K–3)
Tortilla Factory, by Gary Paulsen (K–3)
Turkey for Thanksgiving, by Eve Bunting (K–3)
The Vegetable Garden, by Douglas Florian (K–3)
The Very Hungry Caterpillar, by Eric Carle (K–3)
The Victory Garden, by Lee Kochenderfer (3–6)
Weslandia, by Paul Fleischman (K–4)
What About Ladybugs? by Celia Godkin (K–3)
What Lives in the Garden? by John Woodward (3–6)
Wonderful Worms, by Linda Glaser (K–3)
Yes, We Have Bananas! Fruits from Shrubs and Vines, by Meredith S. Hughes (5–8)

02-005 202-1950-178 12-02 3M